Saluting Our Grandmas

Saluting Our Grandmas
Women of World War II

Col. Cassie B. Barlow, USAF (ret), and Sue Hill Norrod
Foreword by Congressman Michael R. Turner

PELICAN PUBLISHING COMPANY
GRETNA 2017

The word "Pelican" and the depiction of a pelican are
trademarks of Pelican Publishing Company, Inc., and are
registered in the U.S. Patent and Trademark Office.

Parts of chapter 4 are adapted from *Home Sweet Home Front: Dayton During World War II* (2013) by Curt Dalton, reprinted with permission. Chapter 5, by Janet Butler Munch, was originally published in the *Bronx County Historical Society Journal*, 30:1, Spring 1993, and has been reprinted with permission. Parts of chapter 7 likewise written by Janet Butler Munch and originally published in the *Bronx County Historical Society Journal*, 30:1, Spring 1993, are reprinted with permission. Chapter 8 is reprinted with permission from *Home Sweet Home Front: Dayton During World War II* (2013) by Curt Dalton. Chapter 13 contributed by Terry Lee Harmon. Chapter 15 contributed by Francoise Bonnell.

Library of Congress Cataloging-in-Publication Data

Names: Barlow, Cassie B., author. | Norrod, Sue Hill, author.
Title: Saluting our grandmas : women of World War II / Col. Cassie B. Barlow,
   USAF (ret), and Sue Hill Norrod ; foreword by Congressman Michael R.
   Turner.
Other titles: Women of World War II
Description: Gretna, LA : Pelican Publishing Company, [2017] | "Mail Call"
   Cards — Asking Mom to go on the Honor Flight — Early days of World War
   II — Rationing — Making WAVEs in the Bronx: The story of the US Naval
   Training School at Hunter College — Train ride to New York City — Boot
   camp and Hunter College, 1944 — Sugar Camp and the Bombe — Naval Air
   Station, Memphis, Tennessee — Honor Flight experience — The origin of
   the Honor Flight Network — A view of History: Women and Military Service
   — WASPs (Women Air Force Service Pilots) — Nurses in World War II —
   WACs (Women's Army Corps) — The Call to Service. | Includes
   bibliographical references and index. | Audience: Grades 4-6. | Audience:
   Ages 8-12.
Identifiers: LCCN 2016052343| ISBN 9781455623198 (pbk. : alk. paper) | ISBN
   9781455623204 (e-book)
Subjects: LCSH: World War, 1939-1945—Women—United States—Juvenile
   literature. | United States. Naval Reserve. Women's Reserve—Juvenile
   literature. | World War, 1939-1945—Participation, Female—Juvenile
   literature.
Classification: LCC D810.W7 B344 2017 | DDC 940.54/5973082--dc23 LC record available at https://lccn.loc.
gov/2016052343

Front-cover art by Craig Kodera featuring (clockwise from left) Elaine Danforth Harmon, Martha Miller, Dorothy Mae Wise, and Pauline Norfleet Hill.

Printed in Canada

Published by Pelican Publishing Company, Inc.
1000 Burmaster Street, Gretna, Louisiana 70053

To the life and legacy of Pauline Norfleet Hill (1924-2015)

Contents

Foreword

As proud Americans, we can never forget the sacrifices generations before us have made. Those sacrifices and dedication to our country know no bounds and affect each and every American.

Through the journeys of the women in this book, we are reminded that although we were fighting a war that seemed hundreds of miles away, Americans here at home were hard at work to save the world as well.

We will never forget what these women did to ensure victory in World War II and safety for those soldiers on the front lines. Because of their work, it is estimated that World War II was shortened by one or possibly two years.

This book details the wonderful journey many took to serve our country bravely. These snapshots of American life make us stronger and encapsulate the patriotism we hold so dear.

I invite you to share this book about a time that continues to define American history with your friends and family. In doing so, you will honor the Greatest Generation and spread the word about an awe-inspiring experience—the opportunity for World War II veterans to attend an Honor Flight to the nation's capital and visit the memorial dedicated to their services to bring about world peace.

Congressman Michael R. Turner

Acknowledgments

"Thanks" is an insufficient word for what I owe my parents (Vince and Whilma Rizzo), sister (Anne Fantini), brother (Vincent Rizzo), and my family (Tim and Emma Barlow). Anything I have managed to achieve throughout my career is due to their unwavering support of my every hope and dream. I'd like to thank General Wolfenbarger for being an inspiration to me and many generations of women to come. I was blessed to have served under her command. Thanks to my amazing coauthor, Sue Norrod, for being such a great partner on this journey.

—Col. Cassie B. Barlow, USAF (ret)

༺༻༺༻

I would like to thank my dear family (Jay, Amy, David, and Steven Norrod) who have supported me through the grieving process of losing my mother, Pauline Hill, and through the process of compiling information for this book. I love you all. I would also like to thank my coauthor, Col. Cassie Barlow, for her support and work, which have made this book more than what I had envisioned. It is an honor to have my name on the cover with hers.

I am so grateful to the Navy Operational Support Center (NOSC) Cincinnati Funeral Honors, MA1 Johnny Rudisell (USNR), GM1 Brad Newman (USNR), and YNC Robin Titus (USNR) for performing the flag-folding ceremony at my mother's funeral. I knew this book needed to be written after you leaned down to present me with the neatly folded flag. As you placed it in my hands, you softly told me that you were honored to perform the ceremony for a female World War II Navy veteran. After standing up and returning to attention, you saluted the flag or me, I'm not sure which. I only know that I will never forget that moment and the love and pride I felt for my mother's service. Thank you so very much.

We would also like to thank Pelican Publishing Company, especially Antoinette de Alteriis, promotion director, and Erin Classen, editor, for their encouragement, patience, and enthusiasm in completing the book.

—Sue Hill Norrod

⋅⋆⋅⋆⋅⋆⋅

This book has been a journey that brought together many people who have generously contributed stories, biographies, photos, and their love of the women (grandmas) who did amazing acts with little recognition. Thank you to all the people who have helped to make this book possible. We have been blessed to work with and use the stories from these families and individuals. We would like to acknowledge all who have helped make this book possible (listed in alphabetical order):

Mr. Al Bailey, vice president, Honor Flight Dayton, Inc.

Honor Flight Dayton is the Miami Valley, Ohio, chapter of the Honor Flight Network, serving veterans located in all Miami Valley counties and the surrounding area. Originally (in 2005) known simply as Honor Flight, in 2007 the group began operation as an independent local hub as Honor Flight, Inc. expanded into a national organization.

Honor Flight Dayton's primary objective is to provide every deserving veteran a trip to Washington, DC—free of charge—to visit the memorials built in their honor. Its top priority has been World War II veterans, who waited over sixty years to have their own memorial. In January 2013, they expanded the program to include Korean-era vets, followed by Vietnam-era vets in January 2014. Honor Flight Dayton trains Guardians to escort veterans for a day-long adventure to the nation's capital. In addition to approximately six charter flights a year, they conduct an RV ground-transportation convoy at least once a year for those veterans who are unable to fly.

DAYTON, OHIO

There is no question that providing this trip, a small token of what we can do to help those who gave us our freedom, constitutes

Current Honor Flight Dayton board. Seated left to right: Kelley Cox, Rhonda Risner, Diana Pry, and Janet Wells. Standing left to right: Al Bailey, Larry Blackmore, Jim Salamon, and Glenn Greet.

a health and welfare service for our veterans as they enter their twilight years. Honor Flight Dayton envisions its services will continue strong, depending heavily on community financial support.

Mrs. Jackie Berlean, math teacher, Dayton Christian Middle School, for contributing to the Honor Flight Dayton "mail call" card-writing effort, and for your unwavering support when the book was in its initial stages.

Dr. Francoise Bonnell, director of the US Army Women's Museum at Fort Lee, Virginia, for contributing chapter 15 to the book.

Mrs. Jodi Brown, librarian, Dayton Christian School, for researching photographs and information and being excited about the project.

Ms. Laura Brown, for formatting and typing much of the manuscript.

Mrs. Shelly Crain, retired English teacher, Dayton Christian Middle School, for consulting on the writing and editing of the book, and for bringing the Honor Flight speakers to class and writing "mail call" cards. Without your efforts, this book would not have been written.

Mr. Curt Dalton, author, columnist, essayist, historical consultant, and current visual resources manager at Dayton History, for contributing chapters 4 and 8. Thank you for your generous contributions, which added so much to the historical accuracy of events that occurred in Dayton during World War II.

Ms. Britta K. Granrud, curator of collections, Women in Military Service For America Memorial Foundation, Inc., for generously contributing photos and captions from the Women's Memorial Foundation Collection.

Mr. Paul Gregor, Jamestown head librarian, Greene County, Ohio, Public Libraries, for assisting in initial photo-credit information and being instrumental in making connections for us with Dr. Janet Butler Munch, special collections librarian at Lehman College.

Ms. Terry Lee Harmon, daughter of Women Airforce Service Pilot Elaine Danforth Harmon, for contributing chapter 13.

Mr. Earl Morse, founder of the Honor Flight Network, Inc., for contributing biographical information and personal photos pertaining to the first Honor Flight for chapter 11.

Dr. Janet Butler Munch, professor and special collections librarian at Lehman College of the City of New York, for contributing chapter 5 and a part of chapter 7.

Dean Whiteford, beloved former teacher at Dayton Christian High School and an Air Force and Air Force Reserve veteran, and his wife, **Anne Whiteford**, daughter of Martha Miller, for contributing biographical information and photos for chapter 14.

Chapter 1
"Mail Call" Cards

The little crooked stars and stripes glued on the paper cards were so adorable. As an elementary-school art teacher, I have had many requests from teachers for special projects or supplies, but this request was particularly touching. The handwritten notes inside that thanked veterans for service to our country were so sincere. Some words were misspelled, which only made the notes more endearing. This project was requested by the seventh-grade English teacher, Mrs. Shelly Crain, who taught at my school. She was involved with supporting the Honor Flight Network here in Dayton, Ohio. These cards would find their way into individual packets delivered to veterans during the "Mail Call" portion of their bus ride to different memorials in Washington, DC. I had asked several elementary art classes to make the cards for the veterans.

As I gently looked through the stack of cards, I wondered if my own mother, Pauline, a World War II Navy veteran, would want to go on the trip. It was exciting to imagine how much fun it would be for her to be treated so special. I wondered if I could go as her Guardian and push her wheelchair. My thoughts were quickly interrupted by the arrival of my next class, full of anxious students ready to work on art projects. I quickly put the stack of cards down and welcomed them into my room. When I delivered the cards, I would be sure to ask Shelly about the possibility of my mother going on an Honor Flight trip.

Mr. Larry Blackmore was one of the Dayton Honor Flight volunteers. He would often come to Shelly's classroom and talk to the students about the history behind the Honor Flight of Dayton and the goal of taking as many veterans as they could to see the war memorials in Washington, DC. On the day I brought some of the Mail Call cards to Shelly's class, he had arrived for his presentation. I was able to sit in during the class and see the

Author Sue Norrod looking at Mail Call cards (Author's photo)

photos of the veterans and hear how grateful they were to visit the capital and see their memorials. Shelly's seventh-grade class raised money and made cards to present to Mr. Blackmore before one of those trips. As an Air Force veteran himself, he worked really hard to treat our veterans with respect and honor and make the trip memorable for them. He took photos for the World War II veterans at the memorial, each veteran seated next to a folded flag in front of the fountain. For family members of veterans who had passed away before they were able to visit the memorial, Mr. Blackmore brought an 8 x 10 photo of the veteran and took a picture of it next to the folded flag. He called it "Flags of our Heroes." He made arrangements to do this with a service photo of Shelly's father, who had been stationed in the Philippines during World War II. I thought how nice it would be for Shelly to have a keepsake of her father in that way.

After the presentation, I introduced myself and told Mr. Blackmore about my mother's service during World War II. I asked him about the possibility of her going on the flight and of me being her Guardian. He

Shelly Crain holding a World War II service photo of her father (Author's photo)

gladly handed me paperwork for us to fill out and told me to ask her as soon as I could so they could get her on one of this year's flights. I was so excited! Being able to spend a day with Mom on a flight that many civilians never experience was something I wanted to do so badly. I would talk to her this weekend. Shelly and Mr. Blackmore smiled and seemed so happy for me. As I walked back to my class, I hoped that I could get my mother to go on the trip. She was so shy around large groups of people. I decided I would take a DVD about the Honor Flight trip with me and play it for her. Maybe that would help her to see that the veterans were just like her; many couldn't walk the whole day and needed to sit in a wheelchair to see the sites.

Chapter 2
Asking Mom to Go on the Honor Flight

"I hope she will say yes," I thought while sitting in my mom's living room as I waited for the right moment to ask her. I had brought Mrs. Crain's DVD for us to watch. Mom agreed to look at it with me. It was made so well, with patriotic music and even some music from her era. The testimonies of the veterans show how happy they were to be able to visit Washington, DC on the trip. They seemed to make friends quickly as they shared stories and found similarities from their time in the service. I glanced over at my mom as the film showed many World War II veterans being pushed around in wheelchairs. They seemed like they were having so much fun talking and laughing with the other people on the trip. Some of the World War II veterans had flown planes over Europe and had been involved with the invasion during D-Day. Their stories were so interesting. Many veterans were from other conflicts, such as the Korean War or Vietnam. They were from all the branches of the military and proudly wore hats that identified their service. In the airport as they arrived back home, many veterans were brought to tears by the overwhelming show of honor and appreciation by servicemen and women and family members who welcomed them home with flags and signs. I could easily see that it was an experience they would cherish for the rest of their lives.

When the DVD was over, I told my mom about Mr. Blackmore and the Honor Flight that was leaving from Dayton International Airport. I asked her if she would like to go.

She shook her head and said, "No, Sue."

"Mom, I could be your Guardian and could push you in a wheelchair that they provide if you get tired, and I would be with you the entire trip."

She looked over at me and said, "This is not meant for me. I wasn't an officer and I didn't go overseas. I didn't go through what the men did. This is for those who fought and were shot at."

I was afraid of this moment and remembered a quote I had heard during Mr. Blackmore's presentation that helped all veterans see that their service was valuable and deserved honor.

I said, "Mom, when you signed up for the Navy, you gave Uncle Sam a blank check, and you were willing to go wherever our country needed you to go. That took courage and bravery. That is the reason why you and other veterans like you deserve to be honored on a trip like this."

I walked over to the hall closet and pulled out her old photo album with pictures of her with the friends she made during training at Hunter College and with those she shared her barracks with at the Naval Air Station in Memphis, Tennessee. We looked through the photos together before I said, "Just think about it."

Reaching over to a plastic shopping bag I had kept out of sight, I pulled out a cap and handed it to her. It was a black World War II veteran cap

Pauline (right) with two friends from the Navy
(Author's photo)

Photo of a 1940s train on an elevated track in Dayton, Ohio (NCR Archive at Dayton History)

that I had bought for her. Her face lit up as she held it and asked, "Where did you get this?"

"At the Air Force Museum, and only World War II veterans can wear them," I replied. I gently put it on her head and bent down to kiss her on the cheek. "Bye, Mom, I'll see you later. Mom, just think about going." I gathered up my bag and purse and walked out the door, leaving her with a smile on her face as she looked at the cap in her hands.

As I walked to my car, the thought occurred to me that I should see if Mom would go if Uncle Earl or Uncle Ed would go also. They had enlisted before she did, and maybe we could work things out with Mr. Blackmore for the three of them to go together. I would call my cousin Lori to help me get Uncle Earl on board. If anyone could get this ball rolling, Lori could. She was so organized and often helped out with our family reunions. I would call her right away!

As the car drove away, Pauline turned the cap over in her hands and put it on the couch beside her. Looking at the photos in the album, she wondered what had happened to all of her old friends. She put the album on her side table and leaned her head back against a cushion. Images of barracks and planes, hangars and friends at the Naval Air Station still lingered in her memory. As she drifted off to sleep, she remembered her feelings as a young woman riding the train to Dayton, Ohio. She could still see her mother's face and the sight of her younger brothers as she said goodbye and walked toward the train station at the bottom of the hill. These memories were so vivid, she fell asleep dreaming about the train.

Chapter 3
Early Days of World War II

Pauline gathered up her suitcase and purse as the train came to a stop in Dayton, Ohio. The Union Station was busy with travelers and porters helping people on and off the trains. The building echoed with travelers buying tickets or saying goodbye to a loved one. Many servicemen were carrying their bags, heading toward their assignments or arriving home on leave.

The station had a USO (United Service Organization for National Defense) lounge for soldiers to rest between trains. Pauline would often see soldiers reading magazines, using telephones, or just resting with a cup of coffee, doughnuts, and cookies that the hostesses provided. There was even a dormitory on the second floor of the station where the tired soldiers could rest between stopovers. Cots were provided with cards that the soldiers would fill out and give to the Military Police, who made sure they didn't oversleep and miss their departure. Pauline enjoyed the sounds of the busy train station and would look at each soldier as someone's brother or son in route for an assignment to serve his country during this critical time. Oh, how she wanted to do her part! More and more posters were hung up asking women to sign up for the WACs (Women's Army Corps) or for the WAVES (Women Accepted for Volunteer Emergency Service), the women's branch of the United States Naval Reserve. Pauline would always linger at the WAVES poster since her own brothers were serving in the Navy. She admired their uniforms and wondered if she herself could possibly sign up to serve her country as a WAVE when she turned twenty.

As the train pulled away from the station, she collected her suitcase and walked to the apartment she shared with her sister, Lucille, and young Aunt Maudena. She traveled often by train from her mother's house in Somerset, Kentucky, to Dayton. Her mother was a widow with three boys still living at home. Pauline and her sisters, Lucille and Ruth, would often ride the train home to visit and bring gifts and money to help them. It was so easy and such an enjoyable way to travel safely. Her home in Somerset was only one block from the train depot. She could eat breakfast with her mother and her younger brothers and then walk down the street to the depot with her suitcase. There she could wait for the train that went to Dayton via the Union Station in Cincinnati, Ohio. Sometimes the train would stop in Cincinnati to pick up additional passengers. She could usually be back in Dayton by supper time. At nineteen, she had become so accustomed to using the trains, and she cherished her independence.

Dayton was quite different from her small hometown. Everyone dressed up to shop downtown at the local department stores. At Donenfeld's, an upscale women's clothing store, the clerks even wore white gloves. Her favorite place to shop was Rike's on the corner of 4th and Main Streets. It had the most wonderful storefront displays, especially at Christmas. She walked to her apartment and began to unpack and get ready for work the next day. She always read the paper to see what had happened in the news while she was away. The ritual was a habit that she started after Earl and Ed had joined the Navy. She was always on the lookout for news from the Atlantic involving ships and submarines

Wright Field was always featured in the *Dayton Daily News*. It was filled with servicemen and WACs and engineers. On July 9-10, 1943, the ten-men crew of the famous Flying Fortress airplane *Memphis Belle* visited Dayton. The stopover included a speech at the NCR (National Cash Register). The mission was to raise morale in the Dayton community as rationing, volunteer work, and buying war bonds were constantly in the news. Life in Dayton was changing drastically to help the war effort. Since the war had started, many small companies were making military supplies and shipping them overseas. Dayton companies had retooled almost overnight to produce war materials. Companies that made cash registers, washing machines, or car parts turned into companies that produced bombs, bullets, gun carriages, and airplane parts. NCR was the first Dayton company to earn the Navy "E" flag. The "E" stood for Excellence in wartime-material production. Later, companies such as Frigidaire and Delco Products received their "E" flags.

The ten-man crew of the Memphis Belle *(NCR Archive at Dayton History)*

The country needed workers desperately but would still screen each applicant thoroughly before hiring them. Billboards as well as local radio stations advertised the need for women to join the workforce outside of the home so Dayton could meet labor demands. A recruiting campaign was begun that focused on women. The Dayton War Manpower Committee created a new billboard each month to convince women to fill the jobs left by the men who went to war. Cards were even mailed to every home in Dayton, and the Montgomery County area asked women eighteen years and older to register so that the Dayton office of the War Manpower Commission would have a good idea of the working capacities of the women in the county.

With all the defense facilities based in Dayton, the fear of air raids and spies was high. After a thorough background check, Pauline had easily found a job working for a sporting-goods company called MacGregor, which now had converted to making supplies that went into Army packs for the military. Day nurseries were created for moms who entered the labor force. Women who had never worked outside of the home before

A Manpower Committee billboard (NCR Archive at Dayton History)

UNITED STATES OF AMERICA
WAR MANPOWER COMMISSION
UNITED STATES EMPLOYMENT SERVICE   Serial N⁰ 99886

REGISTRATION OF WOMEN FOR WAR WORK

Are you working for pay? Yes ☐   No ☐   If yes, list name and address of company ....

1. Name (print) .... (Last) .... (First) .... (Middle)
2. Address (print) .... (Street and number) .... (City or Town)

3. Telephone No. where you can be reached: ....
4. Age.......... Height.......ft.........in. Weight...........lbs.

5. Will you be available for war work after Jan. 1? Full time Yes ☐   No ☐   Part time Yes ☐   No ☐
6. If you accept war work, will outside care be required for your children? Yes ☐   No ☐
7. Enter in each block the number of children in each group— Under 2 years | 2 to 5 | 6 to 12 | 13 and over
8. If unable to accept outside employment, how many children of working mothers could you care for? ....
9. If interested in work, check below the types of work you would accept:
   How much previous experience have you had in this work, if any?
   Factory ☐ .... years
   Clerical ☐ .... years
   Professional ☐ .... years
   Sales ☐ .... years
   Service and Other ☐ .... years
10. Would you accept free training for factory work? Yes ☐   No ☐

11. What is your present occupation? ....
12. Have you applied for work at the local office of the United States Employment Service during the last 30 days? Yes ☐   No ☐
13. List specified skills or training or make any comments you choose in in this space: ....

A Registration of Women for War Work card (Courtesy Curt Dalton)

Women working at Leland Electric (NCR Archive at Dayton History)

worked alongside men on assembly lines. Patriotism and helping the war effort meant working hard and being on time. Billboards and newspaper ads gave instructions for rationing and how to use stamps for certain items that were rationed monthly. The lines could be long to pick up the ration book, but the books were important, since they helped to control how many items a person could buy during war time.

Chapter 4
Rationing

When war was declared, hoarding began almost immediately. Remembering the shortage of food and other resources during World War I, many Daytonians rushed to their local groceries and began buying items they thought might soon be in short supply. Howard Heisterman, president of the Dayton & Montgomery County Retail Grocers and the Meat Dealers Associations, commented that his office had been receiving calls from retailers asking him what they could do to ease the demand being put on them, especially for sugar. Heisterman claimed that the supply of sugar was more than adequate, and there was no likelihood that it would diminish.

Before long, the Dayton Council for Defense was condemning the practice of sugar price boosting. As sugar became harder to find, some Dayton groceries began requiring that their customers buy a specified amount of other groceries in order to obtain sugar. Although merchants were warned that such practices violated anti-trust laws, Hazel Nolan of the Better Business Bureau admitted at the time that it would be allowed to continue until rationing was effective. The practice was too widespread to actually enforce.

Sugar rationing started on May 5, 1942. Every person eighteen years old or older who lived in the Dayton area was urged to register for sugar stamps at their local elementary school. Even people who didn't think they would have any use for sugar were told to register and receive a sugar ration book in case the stamps were used to ration other items in the future. Some citizens expressed concern because they didn't know where the elementary school in their area was located. Arthur Stock, county rationing coordinator, told those people to ask the children in their neighborhoods; they, surely, would be able to tell anyone how to get to the schools.

The conditions for use of the rationing books were stern, with substantial penalties for violations. For example, when a person died, his or her book had to be turned back in to the rationing board. If a person entered a hospital and expected to be there for ten days or more, the hospital authorities were to be given the person's book. Each person in a family was allowed to have two pounds of sugar on hand; one stamp was removed from the ration book for each pound. Penalties for not disclosing the fact that a person had sugar in the home were severe. Violators could be punished by a $10,000 fine, a jail sentence of up to ten years, or both.

Price administrator Leon Henderson warned that the government had adequate powers to restrain any "chiselers" who didn't abide by the sugar rationing regulations. "A few chiselers can do a great deal of harm both to the operation of rationing and to the moral of the country," Henderson said in a news conference. "The country is in no mood to let chiselers get away with it. Our policy will be to hit chiselers and hit them hard and fast."

As important as it was, sugar was not the first resource to be rationed.

A poster encouraging rationing (National Archives and Records Administration)

Before sugar rationing was put into effect, the country was working to conserve rubber. On January 5, 1942, the rationing of rubber began. Federal rubber rationing immediately prevented about 90 percent of the users of motor vehicles from obtaining new tires. Those who felt the effects of this rationing the most were companies who made home deliveries of bread, milk, and packages. Although 75 percent of the rubber produced at the time was used in the production of tires, the other 25 percent was used to make about 50,000 miscellaneous products such as footballs, golf balls, rubber bands, toys, suspenders, and bathing caps. Manufacturing of rubber bands and erasers was immediately prohibited. The government estimated that from those two items alone, over 8,000,000 pounds of rubber could be diverted towards more urgent needs, such as tires for jeeps and airplanes.

Daytonians took the rationing of rubber good-naturedly, at least at first. Articles in the local newspaper told of horses and carts with wooden wheels being used to deliver milk, just as they had before the automobile took over the job. Jack Davis, president of the Dayton Retail Solid Fuel Institute, reported that no more deliveries of less than a ton of coal would be made so as to save trips. He also requested that customers not ask for their deliveries to be made during a specific time of day so that orders could be consolidated for any particular area.

In less than two months, deliveries by stores had decreased to every other day. Many packages to suburban areas were sent by parcel post or express. The curtailment was designed to save rubber tires and metals and mechanical equipment used in the delivery of packages. The public was called upon to help with the conservation movement by carrying home as many packages as possible.

The first passenger-car tire inspection began in Dayton on December 1, 1942. All vehicles had to have their tires regularly inspected by an authorized OPA (Office of Price Administration) inspector. Each vehicle was given a tire-inspection record to keep with the car. In addition to recording each tire inspection, it documented the numbers on the car's tires in order to stop people from hoarding tires. At the same time, the government put a freeze on the sale of new automobiles, and Dayton auto dealers prepared to tighten their belts. Dayton divisions of General Motor

IT'S SMART and patriotic for every driver to make his car and tires LAST AS LONG AS POSSIBLE. The Dayton Area Ride-Swapping Plan provides a simple, sure, money-saving way of doing this. Read details inside.

SAVE THIS FOLDER! It contains your Registration Card and also provides space for keeping valuable records regarding your car, your tires and your ride swapping arrangements.

DAYTON AREA RIDE - SWAPPING PLAN
MAYOR'S EMERGENCY COMMITTEE ON TRANSPORTATION
HEADQUARTERS OFFICE: 534 MUNICIPAL BLDG. . . . HEMLOCK 8339

★ ★ ★ ★ ★ ★ ★ ★ ★ ★ ★ ★ ★ ★ ★ ★

A Dr. Seuss illustration is used to advertise the Dayton Area Ride-Swapping Plan (Courtesy Curt Dalton)

This poster was displayed to encourage people to walk and save tires (National Archives and Records Administration)

took stock of the effects of the production stoppage, which seriously affected four local divisions of Delco Products. More than 50 percent of the company's sales at the time came from automobile parts, particularly shock absorbers. Delco Brake Division and Inland Manufacturing were also hard hit, as was the smaller Moraine Products Division, whose products included bearing for automobiles.

S. J. Burns, a Lincoln-Mercury dealer distributor in Dayton, voiced the general sentiment of Dayton motor-car dealers when he said, "We have been expecting something like this. It will be hard, but it is part of the emergency and we'll go along, of course." As for his used cars, since there was no rationing on their sales, he expected "no trouble whatever" in selling them.

Food and drinks were also added to the rationing list. When it was reported that coffee rationing would begin in Dayton on November 30, 1942, people rushed to get in line at their local grocery stores to buy as much as they could. Bogart's, a grocery in the Arcade, limited its customers to fractions of a pound of coffee in an effort to make sure everyone was served. Even so, it was estimated that a third of Dayton's coffee drinkers didn't get the mocha they wanted before it dried up.

When the rationing began, anyone older than fifteen was entitled to one pound of coffee every five weeks. The reason for rationing coffee came from the wartime strain on ocean shipping. America's coffee supply came from Brazil, Columbia, and other Latin American countries. Many of the ships that once carried coffee to the United States were engaged in hauling materials vital to the war effort.

In March 1943, it was announced that President Roosevelt had decided to drink milk in the morning instead of rationed coffee. "And he's very proud of himself," Mrs. Roosevelt added.

On March 29, 1943, it was announced that meat would become rationed, and it wasn't long before Dayton was facing a meat crisis. Meat, poultry, and fish were at an all-time low due to the city's increase in population. It was figured that between 1942 and 1943 the population had increased in the city by as much as 25,000 people, with an additional 100,000 commuting to Dayton's factories and airfields daily. To make matters worse, farmers could get as much as three cents an egg and had begun letting their hens lay rather than killing them for market.

Many Daytonians began to drive to nearby farms to purchase meat. The OPA had also set a ceiling price on what the farmers and butchers could charge. With the ready market, many of the farmers disregarded the quotas on the amount of butchering they were allowed to do and the prices they were allowed to sell it for. As one local paper reported, many Daytonians knew "they are conspiring with the farmer to pass his quota . . . not caring as long as they get meat. This form of black marketing probably is enjoying the most popularity at the present time."

This got to be such a problem that the newspapers began comparing it to bootlegging during Prohibition, calling the illegal meat sellers "meatleggers."

A poster displays the amount of meat each person was allowed each week (NCR Archive at Dayton History)

Retail meat dealer E. F. Hapner was glad that meat rationing was going into effect. "I'm all for a way to distribute meat properly," he said. "You can see how little we have on hand here. All day long we tell people, sorry, that's all there is. But it rather worries me because I can't think how they're going to do it. As it is, we've been limiting customers to small portions, like small pieces of bacon. We were glad when they rationed coffee, too, because that way we all got some."

In 1943, Daytonians were urged by the *Dayton Daily News* to grow their own meat at home by buying a rabbit hutch and raising rabbits. Instructions were included on how to build the hutch, what breed of rabbit to buy (they recommended the New Zealand White), and how to make a nest box for the mother rabbit and her babies.

Horse meat, which wasn't rationed, was also sold as demands on meat-production facilities continued to outstrip the supply. The *Journal Herald* described the horse meat, which sold for thirty-five cents a pound, as "good as beef and tender as butter."

Daytonians, as a whole, seemed to favor food rationing. "Those of us who have someone in the service can best know the importance of rationing," Margaret Raines claimed during an interview by a local newspaper reporter. "With a grandson among the armed forces at Dutch harbor, I feel that putting up with rationing uncomplainingly is the very least I can do. Those boys at the front are doing their best—why can't we?"

Mrs. Howard Yost agreed. "Actually, I think food rationing is the only fair system of giving food to everyone. And as for hoarding, I think anyone who has the nerve to hoard food should be classed with spies."

In addition to stamps, rationing was facilitated through a system called point rationing. Housewives found the OPA's official chart of more than two hundred point values displayed in every grocery store. OPA ruled that grocers had to place a card, similar to a price tag, on rationed foods or near the place they were kept.

About 125 trained "explainers" were stationed at groceries throughout Dayton to aid the ration-book holders in "spending" their points on canned goods.

Using points for rationing was a little complex to the average citizen.

The line to pick up ration books at Dayton Municipal Court in 1943 (Special Collections and Archives, *Dayton Daily News* Archives, NCR Archive at Dayton History)

Here's how point rationing for food was explained on February 21, 1943, by the *Dayton Daily News*:

"Here's how Point Rationing works"

1. Every man, woman, child and baby will be given the No. 2 book, which will not be used for sugar or coffee. (You continue to use No. 1 book for coffee and sugar purchases.)

2. Blue stamps are for any kind of bottled or canned fruits and vegetables; bottled or canned juices and soups; frozen fruits and vegetables; dried fruits. (Red stamps will be issued later when meat is rationed.)

3. Number on the stamps show how many points each stamp is worth.

4. Letters show when to use the stamps. The year will be divided into rationing periods. All blue stamps marked A, B and C can be used during the first rationing period. A, B, and C stamps cannot be used after the first rationing period.

5. Blue stamps must be used when any kind of rationing processed foods are purchased. (In subsequent paragraphs are listed the kinds of processed foods that are to be rationed. Different kinds of food will take different numbers of points. For example a can of beans may take more points than a can of peas. Of course, the more you buy the more points it will take. A large can of pears will take more than a small can.)

6. OPA will set the points for each kind and size. An official table of points must be displayed by your grocer; and will be printed by the *Dayton Daily News*. Changes in point values will be made by the government from time to time, about once a month. These changes will be posted in stores; also published.

7. The number of points for each kind of processed food will be the same in all stores everywhere.

"How to use your Ration book"

1. Take your No.2 book with you when you go to buy any kind of processed foods.

2. Before you lay down your money, find out how many points to give for the kind of processed foods you want. Of course, prices don't set the points. The government sets the different points for each kind and size, no matter what the price. Remember, the points will not change just because the prices do.

3. When you buy, take the right amount of stamps out of your blue book. This must be done in front of the grocer or delivery boy; and hand them to the grocer or delivery boy. A stamp or stamps must be collected for all processed foods sold.

4. Don't use more stamps than needed to make up the right amount. If the food you buy calls for 13 points, for example, it is better to tear out an 8 point and a 5 point stamp than two 5 point stamps. Save the smaller point stamps for lower point foods.

5. You can take the stamps from more than one book belonging to your household.

6. Every person in the household, including children of any age, has a total of 48 points to use for all processed foods for one ration period. You may use all the blue stamps marked A, B and C from all books in your household during the first period. As many of the blue A, B and C stamps may be used at one time as you wish. When they are used up you will not be able to buy any more processed foods until the next stamps are good. OPA will announce when the next stamps are valid.

7. Anyone you wish can take the ration books to the store to do the buying for you or your household.

The war was on everyone's mind, and slowly the sad news of casualties

A play held in Dayton during the war made fun of the confusion in the grocery stores when food ration points began. With blue stamps, red stamps, and different foods and various sizes taking a different number of points, it's no wonder the man is scratching his head. (NCR Archive at Dayton History)

Earl Norfleet, Pauline's older brother, age twenty (Author's photo)

Pauline's brother Ed Norfleet, age nineteen (Author's photo)

began to make its way back to the city. Many mothers became Gold Star recipients, which meant that they had a son who had been killed in service to the country.

As much as Pauline enjoyed her independence and living in an apartment with her aunt, she often worried about her two brothers in the Navy. She prayed for their safety and wondered where they were stationed. There were many reports of submarines going missing and daily attacks on ships by German U-boats. Gold Stars were going up in the windows of many homes of the mothers of fallen soldiers. Pauline tried to focus on her job, but that did not change the fact that the country was at war. Everyone was doing their part to help in the war effort. Pauline grew more uneasy each day and longed to do more to help her county and bring her brothers home.

In the days that followed, she walked to work past the post office. Above the building was a billboard with a large picture of Uncle Sam pointing at her. The sign said "I want you." Pauline was sure he was looking at her. With each newsreel at the movie theater or newspaper article, she became more and more worried about her county and her brothers.

One afternoon at work, while she was packing up supplies that went into parachutes, she knew what she had to do. She would enlist in the Navy also. She had just turned twenty years old, which was the age the Navy would accept women into service. She gave her notice to her manager and would take the train back to Somerset to sign up at the nearest Naval Recruiting Office to join the Navy as a WAVE.

Pauline was so excited to serve in the Navy. As she began to pack her suitcase, she thought about the nice uniform she would wear and wondered about the people she would meet and where she might go. The next morning, she was on her familiar train heading back to Somerset to enlist.

Chapter 5
Making Waves in the Bronx: The Story of the US Naval Training School at Hunter College

Severe manpower shortages, which resulted from fighting a war on two fronts, forced US Navy officials to enlist women in World War II. Precedent already existed for women serving in the Navy since 11,275 women had contributed to the war effort in World War I. Women at the time received no formal indoctrination, nor was any formal organization established.

There was considerable opposition to admitting women into "this man's Navy" during World War II, and a Women's Reserve had few champions among the Navy's higher echelons. Congress, public interest, and even advocacy from the National Federation of Business and Professional Women's Clubs pressured the Navy into seriously pursuing the establishment of the Women's Reserve. Training women for onshore naval duty, it was reasoned, would free deskbound men for combat.

Elizabeth Reynard, then a Barnard College professor of English, was commissioned by the Navy to explore the design of the program, and she gave the Women's Reserve its acronym WAVES, standing for Women Accepted for Volunteer Emergency Service. An advisory council, chaired by Dean Virginia G. Gildersleeve of Columbia University and consisting of prominent women educators from across the country, helped organize and establish standards and procedures for the WAVES. The advisory council recommended the appointment of Mildred McAfee, president of Wellesley College, as director of the WAVES program.

On June 30, 1942, the Women's Reserve of the US Naval Reserve was established. An enrollment quota of 11,000 was projected: 10,000 for enlisted personnel and 1,000 for officers. Officer indoctrination was given at Smith College, and these women became the administrators and teachers at Women's Reserve schools. Enlisted personnel initially received basic training at Oklahoma Agricultural & Mechanical College (Stillwater),

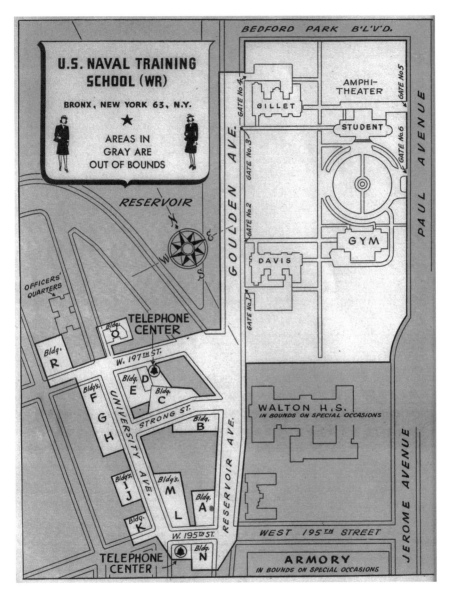

Map of a US Naval Training School (WR) station buildings and boundaries (Courtesy Lehman College, CUNY. Leonard Lief Library, Special Collections)

Iowa State Teacher's College (Cedar Falls), the University of Wisconsin (Madison), and at the University of Indiana (Bloomington).

When it was found that naval indoctrination was inadequate, it was decided that a massive "boot camp" should be established to effect better training and orientation. Finding a site which could accommodate some 6,000 persons at any one time was no easy task. When Texas State College for Women (Denton) rejected the idea of a naval training school, the Bronx campus of the all-female Hunter College was considered. That Elizabeth Reynard knew both Fiorello LaGuardia, mayor of New York City, and George N. Shuster, president of Hunter College, eased matters considerably. The Navy approached both men informally regarding the training school. Having patriotic motivations, both were happy to assist in the Navy's efforts to bring the war to a close. James J. Lyons, borough president of The Bronx, was also enthusiastic about the Navy using the uptown Hunter campus. Indeed, Lyon's own secretary, Margaret Persson, enlisted in the WAVES.

On December 30, 1942, the secretary of the Navy authorized the establishment of a boot camp at Hunter College.

Chapter 6
Train Ride to New York City

The Navy had provided Pauline—and the other ladies who had enlisted—train tickets to take them to New York City. They were all excited and talked nonstop about the adventure they were embarking on. They passed through many stations, and when night came they all agreed to try to get some sleep and be as fresh as they could be in the morning. They were to arrive at the most spectacular train station in the United States: Grand Central Terminal in New York City. Pauline wondered how many movies she had watched with scenes in this historical site. Maybe they would have an opportunity, at some point in their training, to see an orchestra playing in the city. All of the best Big Bands played in New York City at some point in their careers. Many popular singers and entertainers had performed for the WAVES at Hunter College either between performances on Broadway or on their way overseas to perform for the men. Singers like Frank Sinatra, Judy Garland, and Kate Smith had been there. She smiled at the thought of being able to see Frank Sinatra as the WAVES did in a *LIFE* magazine article she had read. She could still picture the pretty WAVES sitting in the front row, so poised in their navy blue uniforms and white gloves. Pauline had read later that they were told to keep their composure and not to behave in an unseemly manner. She wondered if Frank Sinatra ever sang for a crowd of young women who didn't swoon and faint in the auditorium as he serenaded them. These thoughts swirled around in her mind along with images of the Empire State Building and the New York City skyline. Every so often, the blackness outside of the windows would be broken by the lights of small towns as they sped past. She could only sleep for short intervals at a time. At one point close to New York state, the train became an express for the Navy and did not make stops anymore. It just rocked and rattled toward the Big Apple and her new future. Pauline was never afraid or nervous at any point on the trip because she was with her new friends on the train. It felt comforting to be part of this group.

The next morning, the anticipated moment arrived when the group, led by a sharply dressed female officer, stepped off the train and climbed the steps to enter Grand Central Terminal. It was an awesome sight to behold, filled with travelers and echoing voices. It had a high ceiling with streams of light that flooded through the windows. On one end of the terminal was a large mural of army tanks, naval ships, and planes in the sky under a quote: "That government . . . by the people shall not perish from the Earth." It was all Pauline could do to follow the group led by the female naval officer and listen to instructions about taking another train downtown to get to City Hall. She wanted to take in all the details of this thrilling and grandiose scene. After a short ride on their last train, the Navy officer led them up what she said was their last set of stairs. The pedestrians seemed to step aside as they walked into the cool, damp air and the sound of honking cars. Pauline wondered if this was a sight New Yorkers had become accustomed to. In a matter of minutes, they had walked to City Hall, raised their right hands, and were being sworn into the United States Navy as WAVES. The girlish laughter they had shared on the trains together had been replaced with a solemn feeling of pride and fellowship. How proud she was to be part of this group of women and a part of the Navy!

Chapter 7
Boot Camp and Hunter College, 1944

The apartment buildings southwest of Hunter College were turned into barracks to house the WAVES in training. Converted passenger liners had provided the wooden double-deck bunks, lockers, chests of drawers, tables, and lamps. Pauline had been assigned to the third floor of a former apartment building that now looked like an interior of a ship. Each WAVE was assigned a bunk, a locker, and shared a chest of drawers. The women on each floor marched together wherever they went. Often they marched for two hours a day to the tune of Navy songs. The day started with "chow" at 6:00 a.m. (0600), and they would even march in the dark to the mess

WAVES at "chow" (Lehman College, CUNY. Leonard Lief Library, Special Collections)

hall. They did everything together. Their friendship and unity made the strange surroundings home.

A typical six-week program during the period October 1943 to February 1945 included instruction (thirty-six hours) and movies (fourteen hours). Miscellaneous (thirty-two hours) consisted of regimental review, company meetings, war orientation, inoculations, payroll matters, fingerprinting, identification card photographs, orientations, and insurance and bond lectures.

Physical fitness and conditioning of the body were high priorities at the Training School. Having seven gymnasiums, a swimming pool, and an outdoor drill field, the WAVES had ample facilities available on the base for recreation and increasing agility and coordination. Games, such as tennis, softball, volleyball, and badminton, were played, sometimes competitively.

Calisthenics were conducted both indoors and outdoors, weather permitting. Posture improvement, too, received attention in the interest of good health and producing a poised, military bearing.

Determining the recruits were physically and mentally fit for service was an important part of the boot camp experience. Complete physicals were taken, family histories and inoculations were given, teeth and feet were checked, and even psychiatric observations were made. WAVES stood in long "daisy chain" lines for medical examinations, X-rays, and laboratory work. Using a team of physicians and nurses, some 260 recruits were examined each day.

Testing by the Selection Office was conducted in Gillet Hall's auditorium, as well as in Student Hall's "Little Theater." The tests assisted in the classification and assignment process. Beyond testing for general classification, reading, arithmetic, and spelling, the test gauged mechanical and clerical aptitude.

Recreation was built into the WAVES' crowded schedule as a morale builder and included variety show "Happy Hours" on Monday nights at Walton High School, as well as Friday Evening Captain's Concerts. The best in entertainment was made available in the following: singers, concert pianists, ballet troupes, and orchestras. Vladimir Horowitz, Kate Smith, Frank Sinatra, Eddie Canto, Ray Milland, and Jimmy Durante all made appearances. The WAVES also entertained themselves with glee club performances, skits, and shows.

Shore leave gave WAVES a chance to tour Manhattan. The Empire State Building, the Metropolitan Museum of Art, and Radio City Music Hall, for example, were popular WAVE stops. The Automat was always good for a quick, nutritious meal, and riding New York's double-decker buses on a shopping excursion was fun. The Service Women's Center was located at the centrally located Biltmore Hotel. Sponsored and staffed by Kappa Kappa Gamma, the center was a nice place for both officers and enlisted women to meet friends, get theater tickets, and freshen up for an evening out.

Dignitary visits to the Training School were always exciting for the WAVES. Pres. Franklin D. Roosevelt stopped at the station on October 21, 1944, and inspected the troops in a regimental review at the armory. First ladies Grace Coolidge and Eleanor Roosevelt also toured the station. Madame Chiang Kai-shek, too, made an official visit.

At the end of Pauline's training and after extensive aptitude tests, it was found that she would be best suited for the job of machinist mate at a Naval Air Station in Memphis, Tennessee. All of the WAVES on her floor were excited about their assignments and wrote each other's addresses down, promising to write letters to keep in touch. As Pauline packed her suitcase and prepared for the trip back to Grand Central Terminal to connect with the naval train, she paused to think about the transformation she had been through. These past six weeks were filled with so much training, marching, and fond memories with her newfound friends during their shore leave excursions. She would never forget taking the subway to Manhattan and going up in the Empire State Building for the first time. She could have never experienced this without being in a group of WAVES on Liberty. She was sad to see them all head to different assignments, but at the same time her heart stirred with the excitement of a new assignment in Memphis. Maybe she could even visit Mother more often since Somerset, Kentucky, was so close by.

As Pauline's group began their march to the subway entrance in the Bronx, another group of WAVES that had gone through training a year earlier was gaining ground for the Navy in their top-secret assignment back

WAVES marching at Hunter College, WWII (Courtesy Lehman College, CUNY. Leonard
Lief Library, Special Collections)

WAVES in review (Courtesy Lehman College, CUNY. Leonard Lief Library, Special Collections)

Photo of Pauline's section at boot camp, Hunter College, 1944. She is in the second row from the top, third from the right. (Author's photo)

in Dayton, Ohio. They had taken a train to Dayton and then boarded a bus and rode to a place called Sugar Camp owned by the NCR Corporation. These WAVES would work around the clock to maintain a top-secret machine that broke a secret code used by the Germans. The work of these dedicated WAVES would help intercept enemy messages, which saved thousands of British and American lives and shortened the war by at least one year.

Chapter 8
Sugar Camp and the Bombe

It began in 1918, when an eleven-year-old boy by the name of Joseph Desch first saw a crystal radio set in a store. He later recalled that "right then and there I knew what I wanted to do with my life."

Joseph's daughter, Deborah Anderson, says her father passed his first amateur radio license exam in 1926 and spoke fondly of evenings when he would repair radios for fellow students at the University of Dayton.

"Not only had he gained the skill necessary for building and repairing radios, but long before his graduation in 1929, with a degree in Electrical Engineering, he had begun experimenting at home, using various gasses and metal filaments in vacuum tubes blown in his basement laboratory," says Debbie.

After working for General Motors Radio and Frigidaire, Joseph was hired in 1938 to work for the National Cash Register Company in Dayton, to begin the Electrical Research laboratory.

"The move to NCR changed my father's life, allowing him to capitalize on his love of electronics and research."

He began to experiment on ways to develop an electronic counter. A contract was signed with MIT Labs to develop a "Rapid Arithmetical Selector."

"In addition, in the summer of 1940 the National Defense Research Committee had requested that the NCR Laboratory develop electronic defense equipment," says Debbie. "The objective was a counter, operable at one million counts per second. In short, he and Robert Mumma, who had joined him at NCR, were quickly establishing the Electrical Research Laboratory as a pioneer in electrical computation.

"In 1941, their research drew the attention of the Navy as it searched for a company to accept Defense contracts.

"Their initial contract grew into the Naval Computing Machine Laboratory, which opened at NCR on March 9, 1942. The facility, under the command of Captain Ralph Meader, with Joseph Desch as Research Director, was housed in Building 26 on Stewart Street."

Pressure was put on Joseph and his engineers to develop a code-breaking machine. The German military was using a machine, called the Enigma, to encode secret messages. British cryptanalysts, using a machine called a "Bombe," had been successful in decoding these messages at the beginning of WWII. However, in February of 1942, a fourth rotor was added to the Naval Enigma, thereby rendering the British Bombe almost useless.

The readings of these coded messages were very important to the war effort. In 1942, German Submarine U-boats sank more than 1,660 ships in the Atlantic. It was estimated that one in five Allied seamen's deaths were caused by U-boats. Fortunately, the U-boats would communicate with a base on shore to plan their attacks. Desch worked with British scientists to develop the first US code-breaking computer. Six times faster

A WAVE working on the Bombe (NCR Archive at Dayton History)

than its British counterpart, it enabled the Navy to decode the radio communications sent and received by the U-boats. Plans were made and in April 1943, women from the WAVES began arriving in Dayton to help build the Bombes as quickly as possible.

The WAVES were escorted to their new home, called Sugar Camp. John H. Patterson, the original owner of National Cash Register, or NCR, had first opened the camp in 1894 for the purpose of training his company's salesmen. Tents were raised in the spring and summer on land located near the west end of Schantz Road, just south of the NCR factory complex. The land was thickly wooded with large maple trees, where at one time syrup was made. In the 1920s, Patterson built sixty cabins to accommodate his sales force. It was in these cabins that the WAVES stayed.

"I remember how strange and new everything seemed when we arrived in Dayton and how unique Sugar Camp was," says ex-WAVE Jimmie Lee Long. "Living in a cabin surrounded by those huge trees was quite a change from the boot school in the Bronx."

One half of a cabin was separated from the other by a shower. Each side slept either two or three women.

Sugar Camp's thirty-one acres also contained a dining hall, recreation building, social center, baseball diamond, and a large outdoor swimming pool.

"We were delighted with Sugar Camp," says Sue Eskey. "It felt like a little country club. We were more or less like a bunch of overgrown Girl Scouts. We loved it."

The WAVES were given their room assignments, then taken to Building 26 at NCR. It was here that the WAVES began assembling parts for the Bombes.

"At Building 26 we learned how to solder and how to lace harnesses, terminal boards, all sorts of electronic operations that we had never done before," says Evelyn Hodges Vogel. "We were quite adept after a while."

The building consisted of a number of rooms. A male Marine guarded each room.

"We would go down the hill to the NCR building that had been turned over to us," says Ronnie Mackey Hulick. "We had to show identification to get into the building. We sat at a big table and they would bring us a

Two WAVES walk through Sugar Camp in May 1943 (NCR Archive at Dayton History)

graft and a rotor wheel. The wheels were known as commutators. Each commutator had two sets of twenty-six wires. Each wire was a different length and a different color. This was before plastic so these wheels were Bakelite. They'd give us a soldering iron, and we would follow a graft and put these little wires according to the graft. And that would be what we'd do during an eight hour shift. You'd sit there with a soldering iron and wire those little wheels according to a graft. When you'd finish one, they promptly brought you another one."

Secrecy was constantly stressed. A WAVE would never see any other part of Building 26, nor meet any of the personnel, except at Sugar Camp.

"Our work, of course, was strictly secret," says Evelyn Vogel. "We'd never talk about the actual work to each other outside of that room that we were locked in. Nobody had admittance to any of these individual rooms unless they had a reason for being there, and could prove it to the Marine on guard."

Most of the women didn't know what they were building, and none of them dared to ask.

"You didn't question what you were doing," says Jimmie Lee Long. "You just kept that old soldering iron going."

At the time Sue Eskey had an idea of what the rotors' function might be.

"If you had any intuition or deep thoughts about it you could sort of figure it out. There's 26 wires and 26 digits on the wheels and, oh year, the alphabet has 26 digits, too. So you sort of put two and two together. I knew absolutely nothing about codes or anything, but I had that thought. And, of course, I didn't share it with anyone because we were not allowed to talk about anything."

A routine was soon established. The WAVES would march from Sugar Camp, down Schantz Road, then Main Street (Route 48) to Building 26.

"We marched in the street," says Sue Eskey. "We did this because the sidewalk wasn't broad enough. When we marched it was four abreast."

"We worked in three shifts around the clock," says Mary Lavettre. These shifts were from midnight to 8 a.m. to 4 p.m. to midnight. This was a new experience for many of us, as was having a meal at 0230 or 0300 (2:30 a.m. or 3 a.m.)."

. . . On April 5, 1945, at an annual meeting of the Twenty-Five Year Club of NCR, Colonel Edward Deeds spoke of the work being done by the WAVES and NCR for the war effort.

"And in Building 26 for almost three years we have been engaged on a secret Navy project, the full story of which we hope can someday be

WAVES marching to Building 26 (NCR Archive at Dayton History)

Years after the war was over, this picture was taken of Joseph Desch and the laboratory equipment he used to manufacture vacuum tubes for the American Bombes built at NCR (NCR Archive at Dayton History)

told. Whenever our country called, we responded willingly. Whenever necessary, we literally tore the factory apart to get underway without delay. Everybody in this room and thousands of NCR employees who are not here, will always be able to point with pride to what they and their company did to help win the war."

According to Navy records, the WAVES released 50,500 men to sea duty and filled 27,000 other jobs.

The building of the Bombe is possibly the most significant wartime secret that was never compromised. No one knew until the declassification of the records that this project existed. Their success in keeping the secret is something that the WAVES involved with the Bombe project are very proud of.

The world will never forget these ladies or their work. Because of their efforts, it has been estimated that World War II was shorted by one, possibly two years. In 1945, Gen. Dwight D. Eisenhower, in a letter to the British military, wrote that information obtained from intercepted German messages "saved thousands of British and American lives and, in no small way, contributed to the speed with which the enemy was routed and eventually forced to surrender."

Chapter 9
Naval Air Station, Memphis, Tennessee

After mustering out of boot camp at Hunter College, Pauline made the long train ride to Memphis and the Naval Air Station there. These were trains filled with WAVES and often picked up other servicemen. Sometimes after the train began to move, the servicemen would walk from car to car and see if anyone was from their hometown and state. This was an enjoyable time, and many people from the same hometown met each other. Whenever they stopped to eat, they would march to the restaurant designated by the Navy while in route to their new assignment.

After two days, with a few delays on the tracks, the ladies finally arrived in Memphis and boarded a bus to go to the base. By this time they had gotten acquainted and were all excited to finally arrive and apply everything they had learned in boot camp.

The bus took them to the southwest corner of the base, where each WAVE was assigned to a barrack. Pauline met her new roommates and found that several whom she had become friends with on the train were in her building. One of her best friends and roommates, Lois, was from Wisconsin. They were exhausted from traveling but were excited to get unpacked and settled in.

Since Pauline was the tallest in the group at 5'7", she was given the top bunk. She quickly began to make up her bed and put her belongings in the closet assigned to her. The young women chatted away about their assignments and as a group made sure they made it to the mess hall on time. They received more instructions after dinner about their first day on the job.

During their briefing, they were given maps and were told about procedures for meal time and reporting on and off duty. The Naval Air Station had three barracks for the WAVES and twenty-seven buildings for

Aerial photo of the Naval Air Station in Memphis from 8,000 feet (National Archives and Records Administration)

Pauline (left) with WAVES assigned to her barracks (Author's photo)

the men. Other buildings on the base included a skeet range, rifle range, and drill hall. There were so many, Pauline wasn't even sure what some of them were used for. Eventually, she would build up enough time to have Liberty, but there were strict rules about conduct. For example, the WAVES were required to travel in groups while on Liberty.

The Navy had decided that Pauline was best qualified to work with machinery and small parts. She was told that she would report daily to the hangar next to the runway. It was there that she would assist the machinists in the cleaning, repairing, and inventory of parts for the trainer planes that came into the hangar. Most of their repairs were done on the planes' engines. She found out that their air base trained new Navy pilots who would be sent to fly all over the world. She couldn't wait to see the hangar and meet all the people she would work with.

On her first day at work, she wore the assigned trousers and work shirt, just like the other WAVES who were assigned to the machine shop. Many of her other friends had worn their uniform, as they were assigned clerical tasks in offices.

Pauline was met at the door of the hangar by an older man whom everyone called "Chief." He kept track of all the engines that the men were working on and ordered and received parts for the completion of those repairs. She was amazed at the stacks of airplane parts, which filled the hangar from floor to ceiling. Chief was required to know the location and the number of all the smaller parts so that the planes could be repaired as quickly as possible. The hangar was filled with lifts for raising and lowering the engines that were being repaired. There was also an area filled with sanders and cleaning tools. Chief showed Pauline his system and

Pauline and a fellow WAVE after a day at work (Author's photo)

explained that in addition to cleaning parts, she would be trained in the control and inventory of the supplies.

As she was introduced to the mechanics, they smiled and welcomed her and the other WAVES. There weren't many WAVES also working with the mechanics, but Pauline was glad they were there and quickly became friends with them. They helped each other learn the ropes of their new jobs.

As the days progressed into weeks, she slowly took on more responsibility for the inventory and kept accurate records to receive and order needed parts. She loved her job. She worked hard to keep everything neat and clean and kept good records. The Chief had total confidence in her, and she began to feel like the guys in the shop were her brothers. They nicknamed her "Polly."

Pauline had settled into her role in the Navy. She still wondered how her brothers, Ed and Earl, were doing. She would often hear the men talk

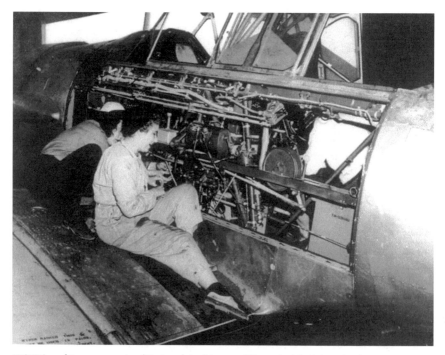

WAVES working on an engine (National Archives and Records Administration)

about what was happening overseas, and she hoped they weren't in the middle of it.

On the base, every mechanic's monthly duty included Flight Time. In some ways, it was a quality control measure to have the mechanic who worked on the plane ride in it after he or she signed off that it was repaired. As a machinist mate, Pauline was also required to have flight time. It was the highlight of her job. She loved getting a chance to fly in the planes that she watched taxi, take off, and land each day. She knew all of the pilots, and it was something she looked forward to. Many pilots really enjoyed taking the WAVES up and "wringing them out." This meant doing barrel rolls and having fun at their expense. Pauline knew which pilots to avoid and managed to find a few who flew nice and smooth. It was so delightful to sit in the open cockpit of the Naval training plane and fly over Memphis or the open countryside. On one such flight, she noticed the pilot was visibly distressed as they were approaching the base to land. He communicated with her to brace for a rough landing, because he couldn't get the landing gear to come down. They circled the base for a long time to use up all their extra fuel, and Pauline could see the fire trucks lining up alongside the runway. Since the landing gear wouldn't come down, they would have to land on the plane's "belly," which could be very dangerous. As they made their approach and the plane began its descent, she braced for a crash—only to be relieved to feel the tires touch the runway underneath her.

The next day, she relayed what happened to the mechanics in the hangar. They had already heard all about the close call and were shocked to learn that she was on the plane; they were sure that she and the pilot would not have survived the crash. Pauline sighed with relief after she realized how dangerous the situation really had been.

She settled back into her routine and looked forward to weekend Liberty, when she and the other WAVES would drive into Memphis or to nearby Chattanooga to do some sightseeing. Some of this weekend Liberty time was spent catching "hops" on planes to Kentucky, which made a quick trip to visit her mother possible. These hops were made available to men and women in the service free of charge. The seating on the plane was not like a regular passenger plane. Sometimes it would be a cargo

A pilot with a Stearman N2S training plane (Author's photo)

A row of planes at the Naval Air Station in Memphis (Author's photo)

plane full of equipment that was strapped down to the floor, with seating and seatbelt harnesses along the sides of the aircraft. Sometimes there were many servicemen and servicewomen on a flight, while at other times she could be the only one flying along with the crew of the plane. On one such flight, the seating was limited, and a young man asked if she would switch flights with him so he could fly home to see his new baby. She agreed and waited for the next flight, only to hear later that the earlier flight had engine failure and had crashed in the mountains. She was so sad as she remembered the look of excitement and appreciation on the man's face when she switched planes with him. Incidents like these reminded her that death could happen at any time, even when you were stationed stateside and not overseas.

Germany surrendered unconditionally to the Allies on May 7, 1945, and President Truman proclaimed May 8 as V-E Day (Victory over Europe Day). Everyone celebrated on the base and in Memphis, but the president asked that the day be one of reverence rather than all-out celebration. The war in the Pacific still had to be won, and the Japanese would not surrender easily. Still, news of victories in the Pacific began to rapidly spread.

Each radio broadcast or piece of news from pilots who stopped over at the base brought new stories about the intensity of the fighting in the Pacific. All of the guys in the hangar were sure that the series of victories would lead to V-J Day (Victory over Japan). Many stories were told over lunch and breaks about D-Day on June 6 the year before. Pauline knew her brother Earl had been on a ship at Normandy on D-Day and told some of the machinists about his experience. He had served on the USS *Cormorant*. Their ship had escorted landing barges that hit Normandy Beach, and they had also shot down two German planes that were firing on the barges. They even sank a German U-boat and picked up survivors from another Allied ship that was sunk by it. Pauline relayed Earl's service with pride and was so thankful that both her brothers had survived the invasion. She enjoyed listening to all the stories that were shared. We were winning the war, and it was just a matter of time before Japan would surrender also.

The Chief approached her one day with a booklet and some paperwork and told her that it was time for her to take her test to earn the rank of machinist mate 2nd class. It seemed like word spread all over the hangar immediately, and for some reason the men decided that they would help "Polly" pass the test. It became fun for all to constantly quiz her. They helped explain procedures and shared tricks to memorize information. Before long she knew the answers to most of their questions: the names of the tools and all the correct procedures for removing components, as well as all the lubricating and electrical procedures. She was in a state of "perpetual study" around all the seasoned airplane mechanics, and she was determined to prove that she could learn everything needed for the exam. The day of the test arrived; the proctor graded it and told her she had made a 100—no mistakes! Pauline couldn't believe it! She couldn't wait to walk into the shop the next day with a big smile on her face.

To her surprise, it seemed like everyone was waiting on her to arrive the next morning. They cheered when she told them she had done so well. Keeping with a Navy tradition, they picked her up and carried her over to a big container of fresh water they had prepared the day before and "tossed her into the drink." This was a Navy custom of celebrating with someone when they passed their test and made rank. Pauline was now a machinist mate 2nd class. Drenched from head to toe, she climbed out of the tub to cheers and laughter and coffee and doughnuts. She was embarrassed at all the attention, and the Chief eventually told everyone it was time to get back to work. Some of the other female machinists were in on the celebration plan and had dry clothes ready for her to change into for the rest of the day. Polly cherished all these things in her heart. She couldn't stop smiling as she realized that this "Band of Brothers" had truly accepted her and the other WAVES as a valued part of their team. She loved them like her own brothers.

On August 6, 1945, the decision was made to drop an atomic bomb on the Japanese city of Hiroshima. Hiroshima was the headquarters of the Japanese regional army and the manufacturing and distribution center for the military. Five square miles of the city were destroyed instantly, and more than 70,000 people died immediately.

Three days later another atomic bomb was dropped, this time on Nagasaki. Nagasaki was chosen due to its steel manufacturing capabilities, and it was also a ship-building center. Almost two miles of this city were incinerated in the flash of another atomic bomb that killed 36,000 people instantaneously.

Everyone huddled around radios, and many businesses in Memphis were at a standstill as the nation waited on any word or rumor that the final moment of the war had arrived. Finally, the voice of President Truman was heard over the radio on the afternoon of August 14, 1945, that Japan had surrendered!

Every city in the United States and those who fought for the Allies across the oceans erupted in cheers at the end of this long, bloody conflict. The war was over! The base burst into celebration, and people were embracing and running to all areas to spread the news. The base immediately issued a shutdown so that both military and civilian employees could join in the merrymaking. The part they had played in keeping the planes flying and training the new pilots was over. World War II had been won! Celebrating continued everywhere on the base, and it seemed that each city in the

Pauline (center) and friends celebrating the end of the war
(Author's photo)

United States took to the streets to mark the end of a long conflict that had left so many grieving over the loss of their loved ones.

Pauline and the other WAVES were given permission to go to Memphis to celebrate with the other servicemen and civilians. People were dancing in the streets and honking horns. Wherever they went, they were offered free food and refreshments, and strangers would hug all the men and women in uniform or shake their hands and thank them for their service. Polly had her picture taken with her two best friends in one of the clubs downtown that offered free food to servicemen and servicewomen. These women were her dearest friends, and together they had served their country. They celebrated and laughed all night long, and as a group they headed back to their barracks, tired and still smiling.

Chapter 10
Honor Flight Experience

Pauline awoke to the sound of her telephone ringing. She had fallen asleep and still had her Navy photo album in her lap along with her new black World War II cap. She slowly rose up off the couch and walked into the kitchen to answer the phone. At eighty-nine she was thankful to still be able to live in her own home. She had a careful system of touching walls and the tops of chairs to steady herself as she walked into each room. She enjoyed her little house with her photos of her four children, eight grandchildren, and three great-grandchildren on display in her living room. She reached for the phone and said hello.

"Pauline, this is Lori. I've been talking with Sue and Dad, and we would like to arrange for him to go with you on the Honor Flight Trip flying out of Dayton."

"Oh, Lori, I'm not sure I want to go." Pauline paused and then asked, "Did Earl say he wanted to go?"

"Yes," she replied, "and you have to go, Pauline. It wouldn't be the same without you, and it will be on our reunion weekend down in Dayton anyway, so everyone can join in on the celebration."

"Lori, I don't think I could manage all that walking."

"Don't worry, Sue will be your Guardian and they have wheelchairs for all the senior citizens to sit and ride when they get tired. She will be with you and Dad the entire day."

After a long pause, Pauline replied, "Well, let me talk to Marcine and see what she says, and I will get back with you."

"Okay, Pauline, and in the meantime we will find a hotel close to the airport and make arrangements. You just have to go," Lori insisted playfully.

Not long after the phone call, Marcine stopped by after work with groceries for her mother as she usually did and heard the entire story. Pauline didn't know that the whole family was in on the plan and had already decided that she had to go. They knew it would be a trip of a lifetime for her; she just needed a little bit of nudging. Earl would definitely not let her stay home!

The day of the Honor Flight arrived, and Marcine, Sue, and Pauline arrived at the Dayton International Airport at 3:30 a.m. There was a table with lanyards, bags, and paperwork to fill out, and they were quickly met by a volunteer to direct them to the area where they would be gathering. Within a few minutes, they heard a familiar, "Well, hello." They turned to see Uncle Earl and Lori walking up with big smiles on their faces. Everyone greeted each other and hugged, and Lori helped fill out Earl's paperwork. The family sat down to talk about Earl and Lori's trip down to Dayton and the hotel they had stayed at and what the day would bring.

Within minutes, many other veterans were pulling t-shirts on over their shirts, putting on their lanyards, and finding the group that they would be assigned to for the day. After some waiting, it was time to move through security. The veterans had a special entry that moved quickly through the scanners.

Marcine and Lori stayed with the group until the Honor Flight participants began boarding at 5:50 a.m. Everyone said their goodbyes, and the veterans and their Guardians headed for their gate.

Marcine, Lori, Pauline, and Earl (Author's photo)

Pauline, Earl, and Sue were assigned to the red group (Author's photo)

Pauline and Earl waiting with the rest of the group to begin moving through the Honor Flight security line (Courtesy Honor Flight Dayton)

These veterans and their Guardians posed for a group picture before boarding began (Courtesy Honor Flight Dayton)

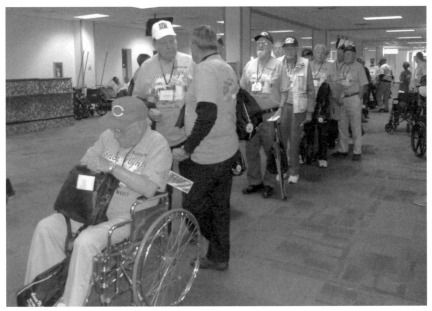

Honor Flight travelers lined up to board the plane (Courtesy Honor Flight Dayton)

Larry Blackmore boarding the plane with his camera (Courtesy Honor Flight Dayton)

Earl seated in the front row and Pauline in the second row between a Korean War veteran and a fellow World War II veteran (Courtesy Honor Flight Dayton)

All the veterans seemed happy and excited to begin the trip (Courtesy Honor Flight Dayton)

Guardians smile for a quick photo before takeoff (Courtesy Honor Flight Dayton)

The flight was scheduled to leave at 6:00 a.m. and land in Baltimore-Washington International Airport at 7:30 a.m. Pauline sat one row behind Earl, who turned around several times before the flight to give her gum and explain how it would help the pressure in their ears during takeoff.

The takeoff went smoothly, and everyone quickly began chatting. They introduced themselves and explained where and when they had served. Throughout the flight, Sue could hear Uncle Earl's voice drifting back to where she sat with the other Guardians. Earl was quite the storyteller, and his memory was sharp. He recalled many details of the D-Day invasion. There weren't many World War II veterans aboard, so many of the younger veterans were absorbed in Earl's stories. Sue smiled as she thought about how perfect a traveling companion Earl was for her mom. Pauline was so shy; now she could just relax and enjoy the ride and smile at the stories she had heard so many times before.

A little over an hour into the flight, the Honor Flight director, Jim Salamon, stood up to announce that no one should worry when they landed and saw fire trucks. The trucks would be spraying water into the air above the plane to make an arch that the plane would taxi under. This was called a "Water Canon Salute" and was a special honor to welcome the veterans to the airport.

The veterans laughed and smiled as the plane taxied under the water spray. The sun shining through the particles made a beautiful rainbow outside of their windows.

After coming to a stop, the Guardians were instructed to be waiting at the door of the plane for their veteran, and to have the wheelchairs ready and waiting if they were needed. As she walked down the jetway, Sue heard a band playing. She quickly glanced outside and saw rows of Navy personnel in their uniforms lining the walls clapping. "Oh, they are Navy!" she said. "Won't Mom and Earl be surprised."

When Pauline and Earl walked off the jetway, Earl led the way chuckling softly and shook as many people's hands as he could. Pauline just smiled and held her head up proudly as I told them that she was a World War II Navy veteran. They all thanked her for her service, clapped, and shook her hand.

When the group reached the bus, the doors opened to a curious group of people dressed in black wearing caps and bandanas. One of the volunteers said they were called the BMI Brownies; they always met the Honor Flights and gave them a motorcycle escort to the World War II Memorial.

Naval cadets and volunteers welcomed the veterans to the airport. Many reached down to shake Pauline's hand while she was rolled by in the wheelchair. (Courtesy Honor Flight Dayton)

As the flight deplaned, rows of volunteers clapped and waved flags, bringing many veterans to tears (Courtesy Honor Flight Dayton)

Our group leader, Carol, made sure everyone was on the bus (Courtesy Honor Flight Dayton)

Members of the BWI Brownies arrived to escort the bus to the World War II Memorial (Courtesy Honor Flight Dayton)

The drive to the memorial took approximately an hour and a half, so the group relaxed and watched an excellent video about World War II and the making of the memorial. Sue gazed around the bus and could only imagine the courageous acts these veterans performed. It was strange that they were so frail now, given how strong they were at one time. Everyone was silent while watching the old footage. It was as if they were looking into the faces of their old friends or remembering the ones who did not make it home. *How blessed our country has been to have men and women to serve and protect,* Sue thought. *Truly, God has blessed America with people like the ones in this bus who did what had to be done to protect the country and its people.* She was so proud of her mother. Pauline sat quietly watching the movie in the front of the bus. She wondered if she would recognize the Navy trainer planes or see her own base in Memphis.

The volunteers wait to get on their motorcycles until the last veteran boards the bus (Courtesy Honor Flight Dayton)

Motorcycles led the procession to the World War II Memorial. The roar of the motorcycles leading the way was exciting, and many pedestrians and motorists glanced over at the bus wondering who was inside. (Courtesy Honor Flight Dayton)

Veterans watching a video about the World War II Memorial (Author's photo)

At 9:30 a.m., they arrived at the World War II Memorial and parked close to the entrance to unload. A man dressed in military-style clothes and holding a sign that read Kilroy Was Here met them along the walkway and posed for pictures with the veterans if they wanted one.

The memorial has a beautiful fountain in the center, with two pillars

Pauline, Earl, and Sue pose with a man holding a "Kilroy Was Here" sign. During World War II, this expression and doodle became popular culture icons. (Author's photo)

on either side. These pillars represent the two theaters where the war was fought: the Pacific and the Atlantic. Around the perimeter of the area are smaller pillars, each with the name of one of the fifty states or a US territory. Metal wreaths hang at the top of each small pillar.

As they made their way down the curved ramp to the fountain, two boys came over and asked Earl about his service and where he was stationed. Earl was glad to answer all their questions as Pauline stared off at the fountain, taking it all in.

Suddenly, four teenagers spotted Pauline's World War II cap and Honor Flight lanyard and came rushing over to talk to her. They were so excited to meet a female World War II veteran. Pauline began telling them about the Navy and being stationed at the Naval Air Station in Memphis. The girls hung on her every word and asked if they could have their picture taken with her. This is the way it was with many veterans. Adults and teenagers alike genuinely enjoyed talking to them and asking them about their service. But these girls were even more enthusiastic than usual, and it seemed they just couldn't ask enough questions of Pauline. They were amazed that she and Earl were brother and sister who had both served in the Navy and made the trip together today.

Earl was glad to answer as many questions as were asked of him (Author's photo)

Pauline and Earl with two boys who were curious about their service (Author's photo)

These girls loved talking to Pauline and learning about her time in the Navy (Author's photo)

These girls gladly posed for a photo with Pauline and Earl (Author's photo)

A band began to play patriotic songs off to one side of the fountain. Pauline enjoyed the music so much. She, Earl, and Sue made their way to the band and saw Larry Blackmore's photo area. He motioned for them to come over and asked Pauline if she would like to have her picture taken with the flag and a photo of her late husband, Bob Hill that Sue had provided. Bob had served in the South Pacific in the Coast Guard and passed away before ever seeing the World War II Memorial. Sue rolled her mother up to the stand next to her father's photo while Larry took their picture.

As the three rounded the other side of the fountain, they saw the Wall of Gold Stars. Each gold star stands for one hundred Americans who lost their lives or went missing in the war. On the wall are a total of 4,048 stars.

Volunteers began walking around the memorial and asking the Guardians to bring the veterans back to the Pacific Altar for a group photo and a flag ceremony. Earl, Sue, and Pauline waited patiently for everyone to arrive.

After the flag passed in front of the veterans, they were asked to give a group salute for a photo. Then they were asked to wave.

Jim Salamon announced that box lunches would be provided back at the bus, and there was plenty of shade and benches nearby to eat them. All were glad and ready to eat and headed back to the bus area.

A band plays in front of the World War II Memorial fountain (Author's photo)

Pauline, Earl, and Sue pose for picture (Author's photo)

Veterans waving in front of the Pacific Altar (Courtesy Honor Flight Dayton)

Veterans take a minute to rest their feet (Courtesy Honor Flight Dayton)

A fire truck created an arch of water for the plane to taxi under. This is called a water canon salute and was a wonderful show of honor for the veterans. (Courtesy Honor Flight Dayton)

The veterans were full of joy as they taxied under the spray of water (Courtesy Honor Flight Dayton)

A rainbow appeared in the spray from the water canon salute (Courtesy Honor Flight Dayton)

The World War II Memorial Fountain (Courtesy Honor Flight Dayton)

Pauline and a photo of her late husband, Bob Hill, at Larry Blackmore's Flags of Our Heroes display (Author's photo)

Sue joins Pauline for a photo with the Flags of Our Heroes display (Author's photo)

Pauline reflecting before the Wall of Gold Stars (Author's photo)

Honor Flight veterans saluting in front of the World War II Memorial (Courtesy Honor Flight Dayton)

Driving by the Air Force Memorial (Courtesy Honor Flight Dayton)

The Iwo Jima Memorial (Courtesy Honor Flight Dayton)

Pauline watches attentively during the Changing of the Guard ceremony at the Tomb of the Unknown Soldier in Arlington Cemetery (Author's photo)

Everyone was mesmerized by the quickness and precision of the Sentinels' movements (Author's photo)

A Korean veteran at his memorial (Courtesy Honor Flight Dayton)

A veteran reflects in front of the Vietnam Veterans Memorial (Courtesy Honor Flight Dayton)

Pauline with her family: daughter Sue (front), grandchildren Steven and Amy (middle), and son-in-law Jay and grandson David (back) (Author's photo)

Pauline and Earl enjoying their lunch together (Author's photo)

The signal was finally given for restroom breaks, and everyone loaded back on the bus. The staff always made sure that everyone was present and this time asked Pauline and Earl to ride up front behind the driver. Sue could tell they felt special and were thrilled to have such a good seat for all the sightseeing.

The next stop was Arlington National Cemetery and the Tomb of the Unknown Soldier. This tomb honors all of the unknown military personnel who have lost their lives in service to our country. It is guarded every minute of every day. Visitors can watch the Changing of the Guard ceremony, which takes place at the end of each shift as a new guard begins his watch. The Honor Flight group was given a front-row seat and enjoyed the ceremony.

At the end of the ceremony, everyone boarded the bus again and drove past the Air Force Memorial, the Pentagon, and the Iwo Jima Memorial. At 2:00 p.m., the bus arrived at a drop-off zone where the veterans could visit the Vietnam Veterans Memorial, the Lincoln Memorial, and the Korean War Veterans Memorial before boarding the bus again. The day had become bright and sunny, and the memorials were full of tourists.

Pauline and Earl with great seats for sightseeing (Author's photo)

Honor Flight veterans and their Guardians enjoyed a perfect view of the Changing of the Guard ceremony at the Tomb of the Unknown Soldier (Courtesy Honor Flight Dayton)

Pauline and Sue in the front-row seat designated for the Honor Flight participants (Author's photo)

The crowd watched the ceremony quietly and respectfully (Courtesy Honor Flight Dayton)

A Korean War veteran talks with a South Korean soldier who stopped to thank him for his service (Courtesy Honor Flight Dayton)

While Earl and Pauline rested on the bus, many guardians volunteered to help other veterans see their memorials. Sue was assigned to a Korean War veteran and pushed his wheelchair through the walkways of the Korean War Memorial. A young South Korean soldier spotted them as they were walking and stopped to thank the veteran for his service. The two were very emotional and talked for a long time about the war.

At 4:00 p.m., the group again boarded the bus and headed to a buffet for dinner. Many were tired and took naps on the way to the restaurant. During this time, the Honor Flight Dayton passed out cards and letters that were written before the trip by the veterans' family members and friends back home. They called it "Mail Call," which was meant to bring back memories of mail delivery in the service. Some of the letters and cards were even written by students, such as Mrs. Crain's seventh-grade English class from Dayton Christian Middle School.

The bus arrived at the restaurant on schedule, and the veterans were ready to enjoy a delicious meal. By this time the Guardians were experienced in getting off the bus first to get their veterans' wheelchairs ready. Instead of taking a wheelchair into the restaurant, Pauline requested to walk and just hold on to her daughter's arm. After dinner, the veterans loaded the bus and began the ride back to the airport.

The veterans continued to read their mail even once they arrived in the airport terminal. They cherished these notes from their loved ones back home.

The mood was happy, even though the veterans were tired. The flight home was quiet, with many of the veterans and Guardians taking naps and talking softly. The end of their highly anticipated trip had arrived. Everywhere they went that day, they had been treated with honor and respect. Many of the veterans had talked about events they had not thought about for many years. Some made new friends on the trip that they would continue to keep in contact with even after getting back to Dayton. And none of them would ever forget their special Honor Flight. It had been a wonderful experience for all.

After a long day, these veterans took a quick nap on the bus before dinner (Author's photo)

A veteran and his son/Guardian smile for a quick photo on the bus (Author's photo)

Veterans began reading their "Mail Call" letters on the bus (Courtesy Honor Flight Dayton)

Veterans treasured letters from loved ones and students (Courtesy Honor Flight Dayton)

Veterans savored their notes from family and friends and continued to read them in the airport (Author's photo)

Veterans and Guardians are ready for their flight back to Dayton (Courtesy Honor Flight Dayton)

The plane landed at Dayton International Airport at 10:30 p.m. Jim Salamon exited first to make sure that everything was ready to go.

Then the procession began. The veterans came off the plane to a great reception by their hometown and loved ones. Active service members and other volunteers lined the hallways. Everyone cheered and clapped for these brave men and women who had sacrificed so their country could defeat its enemies on two fronts. These veterans had lived through the Great Depression, rationing, and boot camps and had stepped out into the unknown for their country and those they loved. Many Guardians cried while pushing their veterans through this "Honor Corridor" to end a fantastic and unforgettable day.

At the end of the procession, many waiting family members held signs for their returning veterans. An Honor Guard stood at attention as they made their way into the main lobby and were greeted with hugs, kisses, and many handshakes by friends and family.

Among those waiting was Mrs. Shelly Crain, the seventh-grade English teacher at Dayton Christian Middle School who first encouraged Sue to ask Pauline to go on the Honor Flight. Mrs. Crain had secretly organized teachers, staff, and students to be at the airport to greet the Honor Flight veterans. Many of them stayed up late in the night to welcome them back.

Service members and other volunteers lined up in anticipation of the plane's arrival (Courtesy Honor Flight Dayton)

The veterans were greeted with smiles and applause as they walked through the airport (Courtesy Honor Flight Dayton)

Guardians and veterans process through the Honor Corridor (Author's photo)

A veteran's family is ready to greet him with a welcome home sign (Courtesy Honor Flight Dayton)

Pauline and Earl were the last veterans to arrive at the end of the procession. This was in part because Sue wouldn't leave Earl, who stopped and talked to many of the men and youth who reached out their hands to shake his. Earl had never met a stranger and was the first in his family of nine brothers and sisters to enlist. He is loved by all who know him—including his oldest sister Pauline, who worried about her brothers so much during those uncertain times in 1944 that she also joined the Navy to help. How fitting that they would go on this Honor Flight together.

At the end of the corridor, Pauline's only son, Jay, reached out to shake her hand. She was so happy to see him and so many of her relatives who were waiting for them in the airport.

Earl's granddaughter, Amanda, ran out to take her grandfather by the arm as he was the last to enter into the "Winners Circle." Lori hugged her father and Pauline as more family members gathered around their veterans.

Sue quickly gathered up her family to pose with their grandma for a quick photo. They had waited a long time for her to arrive. This was their way to honor her service and salute their grandma.

Representatives from the Air Force Honor Guard welcome the veterans (Courtesy Honor Flight Dayton)

Family and friends are excited to have their veterans back home and hear all about their day (Courtesy Honor Flight Dayton)

Mrs. Crain and her students came to the airport to celebrate the veterans (Courtesy Honor Flight Dayton)

Pauline's son, Jay, reaching out to shake her hand (Author's photo)

Earl, the last to enter the "Winner's Circle," is welcomed by his granddaughter Amanda (Author's photo)

Chapter 11
The Origin of the Honor Flight Network

Earl Morse had been caring for World War II retirees and veterans since 1977, when he first joined the Air Force as a medic. When he retired from the Air Force, he joined the Springfield, Ohio, VA (Veterans Affairs). He enjoyed his job, especially getting to know the veterans. After seven years he felt he really knew them well. Many came to the VA because they were on a fixed income and needed the medical services the VA provided for them.

Earl developed a deep appreciation for these humble World War II patriots who literally saved the world. He could only imagine the feeble men in the clinic once flying B-17 bombers over Germany or walking into a death camp to free Holocaust survivors. These men and women are our greatest generation and collectively made Europe, the Pacific, and America free. That just didn't happen; it is not a birthright. These veterans had made it happen. As they returned every three months to the VA, he could see their conditions deteriorating from old age or health issues. He couldn't help but think that they were not appreciated and did not have much to live for.

Then, after waiting for more than sixty years, these heroes finally had a memorial being built for them in Washington, DC. It was dedicated on Memorial Day 2004, and there was great excitement in the little VA clinic. The veterans themselves were grinning from ear to ear and held their heads just a little bit higher. All of them wanted to go see the memorial and thought that a son or daughter, or perhaps their VFW (Veterans of Foreign Wars) or DAV (Disabled American Veterans) posts, would organize a trip.

Earl usually saw his seventy-year-old to ninety-year-old patients every three to six months because of their health issues. At each visit he would ask if they had been to see their new World War II Memorial. That's when they would break eye contact and look at the ground, and the smiles would fall from their faces. Their excuses ranged from their kids being too busy to health problems to family financial issues to their spouses being sick, etc. It was painful for these veterans to realize that they were not going to get any richer, healthier, or more able to organize a trip as the time passed. Reality was setting in that they were never going to visit their memorial. Earl decided to quit asking the question because it was just too painful to see the looks on his patients' faces. By December of 2004, he had seen all three hundred of his World War II veteran patients at least once since the memorial had been built, and not one of them had visited it.

They were his patients, and they were dying. One night Earl couldn't sleep for thinking about the veterans. He had always been taught by his parents and his pastor to do whatever was in his ability to help people and show them God's love, whether that was taking a bag of groceries to a needy family or doing random acts of kindness. He now knew what he had to do. He was a private pilot and a member of the Aero Club at Wright-Patterson Air Force Base (AFB) in Dayton. He himself would fly the most-needy veteran who could not make it on his own to see the World War II Memorial. Earl's dad, a Vietnam veteran, was an excellent copilot. They would often fly short trips to Put-in-Bay, or to Cleveland to watch the Browns or the Indians play. Earl decided he would talk to his dad the next day.

After work the next day, he met with his father, explained his idea, and asked if he would split the $350-$400 aircraft rental fee and help him fly a couple of World War II veterans to see their memorial. Earl explained that if they didn't do it, these veterans would probably never have an opportunity to see the memorial. His father agreed to his plan.

The next week, Earl explained the trip to his first veteran, Leonard Loy. Earl came into the office and asked Mr. Loy if he had any plans to visit his memorial. He saw the same dejected expression he had seen so many times before, the face of a veteran confronting the impossibility of making the journey. Earl then told him that he was a private pilot and that he and his dad would be flying out to Washington, DC to visit the Vietnam, Korean, and World War II Memorials. They would fly Mr. Loy out there if he wanted to go, for free. Earl paused, waiting for an answer. He wasn't ready for him to start crying. But Mr. Loy was so touched that tears fell from his eyes. After he stopped crying, Earl wrote down Mr. Loy's name and phone number and told him that they would get back with him later.

A nurse had seen an emotional Mr. Loy come out of the office and asked Earl if everything was all right. Earl explained to her what happened, and then she started to cry also. She asked if she could invite another World War II veteran to fill that final seat. Earl told her she could. When she asked the veteran a few days later, she got the same response Earl did; the veteran began to cry. The nurse told Earl what had happened.

At that point, he knew that this effort meant a lot more to the World War II veterans than he had imagined. There was absolutely no turning back at that point. They were definitely going to make this happen. But Earl had no idea how big it was going to get.

Since the first flight required that they get the approval of the Aero Club manager, Earl called to ask permission to fly from Wright-Patterson AFB to Andrews AFB in Maryland. Earl told the manager about the new World War II Memorial, the more than three hundred World War II veterans who would never be able to visit it, and how the two veterans they invited on the trip had cried.

The manager, Ron Smith, was a Marine veteran who served three tours in Vietnam. After he heard Earl's story, there was a long pause over the phone. Earl thought he had lost the phone connection, but he later learned that Ron, like all who had heard the plan before him, was crying, trying to compose himself. He told Earl, "Not only can you do it, this is a great idea. I want you to bring this up at the next Aero Club safety meeting." The club had meetings every month, and about 150 pilots attended every meeting. During Earl's proposal at the next meeting, he explained his idea and asked for two things of anyone who wanted to help:

1.   The veterans would fly for free. The volunteer pilots would have to fund the entire aircraft rental fee.

2.   All of the pilots gathered were active-duty or retired military. They had to promise not to use the trips to fly out of Andrews to meet their buddies. The entire focus—all of their efforts and concerns—would be to care for the veterans and transport them safely. There would be absolutely no personal agendas that day. The pilots would be considered the veterans' "guardians" for the day.

Eleven pilots volunteered on the spot that night, so they instantly had a program. As the months went by, they recruited more and more veterans, as well as more and more pilots, and the program grew dramatically. Still, the growth was not big enough or fast enough. At the end of the first year, they had only transported 137 World War II veterans to DC, but they had more than eight hundred names on the waiting list. Over sixty veterans had passed away in the meantime, anxiously waiting to go. They wrapped up their flying season with hundreds of calls. Veterans asked when they would get to go on a flight; occasionally spouses of veterans asked them to take their husband's or wife's name off the list, for they had died.

Each and every one of those conversations kept Earl up at night. He had hundreds of names on the waiting list but no money and no prospects for the necessary funding. There was no one else in the nation doing this. He was also still working full-time at the VA. Eventually exhaustion set in, and management at the VA began questioning his motives. He was even investigated by management and pressured not to continue the flights.

Before the first Honor Flight, May 21, 2005. From left to right: Chuck Daily, Honor Flight pilot; Leonard Loy, first World War II veteran asked by Earl Morse to see the World War II Memorial; Earl Morse. (Courtesy Earl Morse)

A single Piper Arrow takes off as the very first plane of the first Honor Flight (Courtesy Earl Morse)

A group photo from the first Honor Flight taken at the World War II Memorial. The veterans are in the front and the pilots are in the back. (Courtesy Earl Morse)

The logo of the national Honor Flight Network (Courtesy James A. McLaughin, chairman of the board, Honor Flight Network)

This led Earl to quit his job at the VA and devote his full effort to Honor Flight. He knew he had made the right decision as doors began to open and volunteers and donations began to pour in. Today, the Honor Flight Network has transported more than 170,000 World War II, Korean War, and Vietnam War veterans from more than 140 cities across the country to their memorials, and they all fly for free.

Chapter 12
A View of History: Women and Military Service

It isn't just my brother's country, or my husband's country, it's my country as well. And so the war wasn't just their war, it was my war, and I needed to serve in it.
—Maj. Beatrice Hood, US Army, World War II

Women have come a long way since the first woman started serving in the United States military. In fact, all women who have served in the military now have a memorial to their service at the entrance to Arlington National Cemetery. Called the Women in Military Service for America Memorial, it was dedicated in late 1997 in front of thousands of people who came to share in the historic event.

In the early days of women's military service, during the Revolutionary War, women who were passionate about serving could only do so by hiding their gender. Most women at this time were supposed to stay home and take care of their family while the men in the family fought the war. In addition, schools were not open to girls, and very few women worked for pay. Women could not officially be soldiers, but that didn't stop the first courageous woman from serving.

Deborah Sampson was born in 1760 in Massachusetts, very close to where her pilgrim relatives had settled 140 years earlier. Her family was very poor, so they were servants on another family's farm. The Revolutionary War had been ongoing for several years when Deborah, who was in her early twenties, decided she wanted to join the fight. She cut her hair very short, dressed like a man, and headed into town to enlist. She must have done an amazing job with her disguise since nobody noticed. She even used a man's name (Robert Shurtlieff) when she signed up to serve.

Deborah fought right alongside the men in her unit. All of the men in her battalion called her Bob. At one point during her service, she was wounded and tried to take care of herself so she wouldn't have to visit the doctor and potentially have her secret revealed. Unfortunately, she later became sick with a fever, so a doctor had to examine her and listen to her heart. Of course, he quickly determined that she was a woman in men's clothes. This ended her career in the military. When Deborah recovered from her illness, she was given an honorable discharge and sent back to her home. Later in her life, during a speech she delivered about her wartime service, she said "a new scene and a new world opened to my view."

There are several accounts from the Revolutionary War of other women similarly dressing as men and serving until they were discovered. In addition to the small number of women who fought on the Revolutionary War battlefields, there were an estimated 20,000 female battlefield aides who helped the men load guns and cannons, cared for the wounded, and conducted many other noncombat jobs. The more women who helped in noncombat roles, the more men who were available for combat.

Drawing of Deborah Sampson from The Female Review: Life of Deborah Sampson, the Female Soldier in the War of Revolution, *circa 1797* (Massachusetts Historical Society)

Statue of Deborah Sampson at the Sharon Library, Sharon, Massachusetts (US Army Women's Museum)

After the British surrendered in 1781 at the end of the Revolutionary War, many women hoped that the new United States government would allow for equal rights since so many women helped during the war. But that wouldn't happen for nearly another 140 years.

The next opportunity for women to serve in a military conflict was the Civil War. The rules disallowing women to serve had not changed since the Revolution. But also as during the Revolution, many women still rushed to help in some way. More than 10,000 women cared for the sick and wounded as nurses. Some famous nurses from this era include Clara Barton, who founded the American Red Cross, and Louisa May Alcott, who wrote the well-known novel *Little Women*. There were also several female doctors who served their country during the Civil War. One such woman was Dr. Mary Walker, the first woman to be awarded the Congressional Medal of Honor. Today, she remains the only woman ever to receive that award.

Hundreds of women wanted to take up arms to fight for their country during the Civil War. Since they were still not legally allowed do so, they followed the family practice of dressing up as men and adopting men's names. One example of such a woman is Sara Emma Edmonds. She joined a Michigan Army unit under the name Franklin Thompson. Sara was also eventually discovered when she became sick and had to be examined by a doctor. When the end of the war drew close, soldiers were needed badly. Some Southern women responded to this need by creating their own guard units. These units were not officially part of the Confederate Army, but they were there to defend their homes in case of an attack while their men were away.

The next conflict in which America was involved was the Spanish-American War. Army officials were more diligent in screening soldiers during this war and thoroughly examined everyone very carefully. Army doctors were directed to create a full body diagram of each soldier. On this diagram, every scar and mark on the soldier's body was recorded. This new technique helped Army officials in two ways. First, it helped them catch people who were trying to re-enlist to earn soldier's pay after being discharged under less than honorable conditions. Second, this new procedure made it impossible for women to enlist and hide their gender.

An all-female Civil War guard unit (National Archives and Records Administration)

The good news in this conflict is that women were welcomed to serve the Army as civilian nurses. These nurses did such a great job that the Army decided to create its first female unit: the Army Nurse Corps. The Navy did the same thing soon thereafter. Equal treatment for these women in the service was still many years away. For example, they were not allowed to have military titles, such as lieutenant. With this said, these two new units were historic nonetheless.

A turning point in women's US military history came with World War I. For the first time, women were allowed to be full, official members of the United States Navy. They held the same rank and duty titles and were paid the same as their male counterparts. A twenty-year old woman from Pennsylvania, Loretta Walsh, was the first woman to sign up with the Navy; 12,000 women followed suit to serve as yeomen in World War I. These yeomen worked in offices as administrative specialists across the US Navy. The reason many women were recruited during World War I was that there was a severe shortage of troops across the United States. The Secretary of the Navy figured that he could free up men to serve on ships if he could get women to help in office jobs. This tactic worked, and many women came forward to serve. The Marines started enlisting women office workers soon after the Navy. Sgt. Martha Wilchinski was one of the first women to enlist in the Marines. She had studied to be a writer at college, so being a Marine publicity officer was a perfect fit for her. She wrote humorous articles for Marine magazines and had publicity photos taken of her to encourage others to enlist.

In addition to filling administrative positions, approximately 21,000 women served as military nurses during War World I. Nearly half of these women served in Europe. Most nurses traveled overseas with the troops, moving their medical tents from one battlefield to the next. Lillian Blackwell Dial, who hailed from North Dakota and was eager for adventure, found it quickly as an Army nurse in France. She was on a mobile hospital team that traveled around Europe. At the end of the war, approximately 290 women received the highest award available to noncombatants, the Distinguished Service Medal. In addition, there were four Army nurses who came under enemy attack and therefore received the Distinguished Service Cross, an award typically given only to those involved in combat.

At the completion of World War I, a few hundred women remained in the military as nurses. For about twenty years after the war, nurses were the only women allowed to serve in the military. All other women, including administrators, were discharged. But two decades later, women were once again counted on by their nation when the United States entered World War II.

In early 1941, Congresswoman Edith Nourse saw world tensions rising and recognized that there may soon be a need for women in the military. She introduced a bill in Congress to create a women's branch of the Army. The passing of this bill was truly historic and momentous for all women. The United States military, fighting around the world, needed all healthy Americans to serve in World War II. The woman chosen to lead the new women's corps for the Army was Oveta Culp Hobby, a college graduate, newspaper publisher, wife of a former Texas governor, and mother of two children. The other services quickly followed the Army's lead. Over 350,000 women served in these units, more than ten times as many women who served in World War I. These women were from all walks of life and many different generations.

Each service had a different name for their female unit. The Navy called their unit WAVES, Women Accepted for Volunteer Emergency Service. The Coast Guard women were called SPARs, a name referring to the Coast Guard's motto, "Semper Paratus—Always Ready." The Marines simply called their women Marines. The Army named their female unit the WACs, Women Army Corps. Even though women were allowed to hold the same rank as men, they could not rise to the top of the rank structure. For instance, there was only one full colonel allowed in the WACs.

The role of women was much expanded during World War II. There were many new specialties in which women were allowed to serve, as long as they were noncombat roles. For instance, women drove and maintained trucks and worked in radar maintenance, radio operations, intelligence, air traffic control, parachute packing, aircraft maintenance, and navigation training. Although the women were not allowed to serve as combat pilots, there was a women's group called the WASPs, Women Airforce Service Pilots. These women were technically not in the military but were hired as civilians and flew many noncombat military missions. Often, these women delivered aircraft to different locations required by the military. In late 1944, the Army ended the WASP program, and women would not fly again in the military for almost thirty years.

The first women prisoners of war were taken in World War II. There were eighty-one Army and Navy nurses serving in the Philippines when Japan took control of the country in 1942. These women were held at Santo Tomas University, which was converted to a prison during the war. The conditions in this prison were dreadful for the women. They slept on the floor, regularly didn't have enough food, and had no medical care. Although there were no female deaths in the prison, many others did not make it through captivity, which lasted several years.

There were unprecedented opportunities for women during World War II, and many women not only took advantage of them but also paved the way for generations to come. One notable example is Grace "Amazing Grace" Hopper, who was a math teacher before joining the Navy. Grace hailed from New York and came from a family of engineers. Her grandfather was a civil engineer who helped build the Bronx. One of her favorite childhood memories was following her grandpa around on

Grace Hopper working on Mark I, the first large-scale automatic calculator and precursor of electronic computers. Here she is a lieutenant assigned to the Bureau of Ordnance's Computation Project at Harvard University, 1941. (US Navy)

Commodore Grace M. Hopper (US Navy)

adventures in New York City, watching him work. Grace studied math at Yale, graduated with a PhD in 1931, and then began a career in teaching. She joined the US Navy Reserve in 1943 and was assigned to a computer lab at Harvard. She then had what she called a "life altering" experience with the first large-scale digital computer in the United States, Mark I. Grace was the one who coined the term "computer bug"; she found and removed a trapped moth from Mark I's inner circuitry. Grace had a critical role in the development of the first commercial computer, called Univac I, and subsequently a new computer language called COBOL. Grace decided to retire from the US Navy Reserve in 1966, but it didn't last for long. The Navy asked her to come back and work on the many Navy computer-language projects in the works. In 1975, Congress passed legislation that allowed Grace to be promoted to the rank of captain, and in 1983 she received a presidential appointment to the rank of rear admiral. She then served for twenty years in the Pentagon in the Naval Data Automation Command. In 2016, Grace was posthumously awarded the Presidential Medal of Freedom, the nation's highest civilian honor.

Another woman who paved the way for future generations was Jeanne Holm, the first female from any branch of the service to achieve two-star

Maj. Gen. Jeanne Holm, mid-1970s (National Archives and Records Administration)

Jacqueline Cochran, early 1940s (National Air and Space Museum Archives, Smithsonian Institution)

general rank. Jeanne was born in Portland, Oregon, and was a trained silversmith. She enlisted in the Women's Army Auxiliary Corps (WAACs) in 1942. Commissioned as a lieutenant and quickly rising to captain, she was in charge of a woman's training regiment. At the end of World War II, she returned to civilian life to earn her degree. She was soon recalled to service during the Berlin Blockade (1948-1949) and was transferred to the newly established US Air Force. Jeanne was assigned to develop war plans in Germany. Soon after this assignment, she was the first woman to be selected for and attend the Air Command and Staff School. From there she was assigned to Naples, Italy, and was responsible for all manpower needs of the Headquarters of the Allied Air Forces for Southern Europe. Jeanne returned to Washington, DC in 1961 as a congressional staff officer and became the director of female personnel in the US Air Force in 1965. In this position, she created many opportunities for women in the US Air Force and rewrote many regulations to abolish discriminatory practices. She closed out her career as the director of the secretariat of Air Force personnel.

Jacqueline Cochran was another amazing trendsetter in the World War

II era. Born into challenging circumstances as an orphan in Florida, she was raised by foster parents and had no formal education in her formative years. In her early years, she worked in a beauty parlor in Montgomery, Alabama, and then moved to New York, where she was a hairdresser at a Saks Fifth Avenue salon. Jacqueline met a wealthy businessman, whom she later married. He encouraged her to pursue her dream of flying, so she obtained her pilot's license in just three weeks in the summer of 1932. Jacqueline achieved many flying firsts as a woman: she flew and tested the first supercharger installed on an aircraft engine, piloted an unpressurized biplane at 34,000 feet while wearing an oxygen mask, and flew in the 1935 Bendix transcontinental race, winning the title in 1938. In 1941, she became the first woman to fly a US Army Air Force bomber across the Atlantic. Jacqueline was a driving force behind the WASP program and was appointed its director in 1943. Because of her personal encouragement and endorsement, over 25,000 women applied to be WASPs. More than 1,000 women eventually graduated from rigorous WASP training and collectively flew more than sixty million miles for the US Army Air Force. Jacqueline received the Distinguished Service Medal for her many years of service to her country. She was later among those who successfully lobbied Congress for veteran benefits for WASPs. She served from 1948 to 1970 in the US Air Force Reserve and retired with the rank of Colonel.

Very few people thought the United States could again be engaged in war so quickly after World War II ended. The United States was involved on the international stage when the communist North Korean government invaded South Korea in 1950. The fighting continued for three years and left millions dead, including 33,000 from the US military. Women had been permanent members of the US military since 1948, with approximately 22,000 on active duty at the start of the Korean War. They played a smaller role in this war then they had in World War II, primarily because fewer US troops were engaged in the Korean War. In addition, it was deemed that only 2 percent of the total number of service members could be women.

Army nurses were key contributors to the Korean War effort. As a matter of fact, nurses were among those first deployed. Capt. Carmela Filosa Hix was one such nurse. She was born and raised in New York City and was the first in her family to attend college. She then graduated from nursing school and quickly began work in a New York hospital. Her parents were first-generation Americans who emigrated from Italy, so being an American meant a lot to Carmela. For this reason, she left the New York hospital in early 1950 to join the Army Nurse Corps (ANC). She spent several years in a Mobile Army Surgical Hospital, or MASH unit, taking care of the war-injured in Korea. After the war, she stayed in the Army for several years, deciding to leave after she had her first child.

Once again, several years after the Korean War ended, the United States found themselves faced with another war, this time in Vietnam. Only a few jobs were available to women in 1959 when the United States began their involvement in Vietnam. By the time the war ended in 1975, the range of jobs available to women in the military had increased. This was primarily because of the difficulty with the draft during this time period and the lack of US citizen support of the Vietnam War. By its end, about 58,000 Americans had lost their lives. Because of the draft, which required men between the ages of eighteen and thirty-five to serve in the military, US officials began to allow women to qualify for more noncombat jobs. Nurses were once again the largest group of American servicewomen in Vietnam, much like the Korean War.

The civil rights movement during the 1960s helped women expand their opportunities for military service even further. In 1967, Congress eliminated the rule limiting the number of women who could serve in the military. When the draft ended in 1973, the US military became an all-volunteer force. This was the point at which US officials realized the need for women in the military. Other rule changes quickly followed, like allowing women with children to serve and allowing women to serve on ships. The skies also opened to women in 1973 when they could train to be Army and Navy pilots; a few years later, in 1976, the Air Force changed its rules as well.

Barriers continued to fall for women. In 1976, the first women were admitted to the US service academies. In 1978, the Army stopped singling out its women by calling them WACs. Other branches had already stopped using names like WAVES and SPARS. Servicewomen were known by the same names as their male counterparts: soldiers, airmen, marines, and sailors. These massive changes across the Department of Defense led to over 100,000 women on active duty by the end of the 1970s.

The Persian Gulf War in the early 1990s was the first major war since many of these new positions had been opened to women. Women earned an unprecedented number of Bronze Stars and Purple Hearts in this war. For the first time in history, they truly fought next to their brothers in arms and blazed critical trails. This was also the first war in which women served with families at home. Families across the United States rallied behind these women and helped care for their children while they were away at war.

In 1991 and 1993, major decisions came out of Congress. First, women were allowed to fly in combat missions, and then women were allowed to serve on most combat ships. In 2014, the first woman graduated from the US Army Ranger course. Today, approximately 14 percent of the US military is female, and they serve in almost every career field. Women have proven that they can contribute in the toughest of roles and are truly thankful to the many generations of both men and women who worked to make women's service possible in the United States.

The first Women's Army Auxiliary Corps (WAAC) unit in overseas service arrives in North Africa for duty in the headquarters of Gen. Dwight D. Eisenhower, commander of the Allied Forces in North Africa, 1943 (National Archives)

WAC and soldier test radio equipment, First Service Command, World War II (US Army Signal Corps photo, Elizabeth [Winslow] Stearns Collection, Gift of Lois M. Bowen, Women's Memorial Foundation Collection)

WAC Tech Sergeant Martha (Stancil) Sugg, assigned to the Central Mail Directory Service, carries mail out of the 7th Base Post Office, Biak, Netherlands, East Indies, 1944 or 1945 (Martha [Stancil] Sugg Collection, Women's Memorial Foundation Collection)

Somewhere in England, Maj. Charity E. Adams inspects the 6888th Central Postal Directory Battalion, only African American WACs assigned to overseas service, February 1945 (National Archives, 111-SC-200791)

American WACs attached to a forward echelon Headquarters operate a portable Signal Corps switchboard in a French wine cellar, World War II (US Army photo, Helen [Braun] Ferrar Collection, Women's Memorial Foundation Collection)

Army nurses, once stationed on Bataan and Corregidor and recently liberated after three years as prisoners of war (POWs) in Santo Tomas Internment Camp, Manila, the Philippines, are on their way home wearing new uniforms, February 1945 (US Army Signal Corps Photo)

Army nurses relaxing outside their tent at a field hospital in Southern France, World War II (Ruth DeLoris Buckley Collection, Women's Memorial Foundation Collection)

Army Nurse Corps flight nurse 2nd Lt. Madge Kirk attends a wounded American soldier, one of many being evacuated by air to the United States from the 57th Field Hospital in Prestwick, Scotland, August 25, 1944 (US Army Signal Corps)

Lt. Ruth DeLoris Buckley takes a wounded soldier's blood pressure, 95th Evacuation Hospital, World War II. Lieutenant Buckley served in North Africa, Italy, France, and Germany with the 95th Evacuation Hospital from 1943 to 1945. On February 7, 1944, she was wounded when German aircraft bombed the 95th at Anzio, Italy. (Ruth DeLoris Buckley Collection, Women's Memorial Foundation Collection)

Army nurses march during basic training, Greensboro, North Carolina, 1944 (Sophie [Peda] Harrison Collection, Women's Memorial Foundation Collection)

Army nurses Lieutenants Sylvia Hamper, Anna (Lance) Fender, Nita Manley, and Ruth Reed slog through the mud, 94th Evacuation Hospital, Italy, World War II (Anna [Lance] Fender Collection, Women's Memorial Foundation Collection)

These four Army nurses are among the first to arrive on Okinawa, May 4, 1945. Left to right: Lieutenants Kifel, Hendeshot, Kennedy, and Plafker (Army Nurse Corps Collection, Research Collection, US Army Center of History and Heritage, Fort Sam Houston, Texas)

WASPs, wearing their service uniforms, pose for a group photograph, Harlingen Army Air Field, Harlingen, Texas, World War II (US Air Force photo, Dorothy [Hubert] Clement Collection, Women's Memorial Foundation Collection)

WASP Betty Jane Williams in the cockpit of a P-40, which she had just landed, on Randolph Field, San Antonio, Texas, November 1944 (Betty J. Williams Collection, Women's Memorial Foundation Collection)

A WASP gets into her aircraft, Harlingen Army Gunnery School, Harlingen, Texas, World War II (US Air Force photo, Dorothy [Hubert] Clement Collection, Women's Memorial Foundation Collection)

WASP pilot trainee Marie Michell, Avenger Field, Sweetwater, Texas, late 1943 or early 1944 (Marie [Michell] Robinson Collection, Gift of Roy Michell, Women's Memorial Foundation Collection)

WAVES march in formation in honor of the WAVES' second anniversary, Hunter College, the Bronx, New York, 1943 (Margaret [Pile] Stockton Collection, Women's Memorial Foundation Collection)

WAVES lower an airplane engine onto a block, Naval Training School, Norman, Oklahoma, July 1943 (US Navy History and Heritage Command, NH86160)

WAVE Gunnery Specialist Third Class Marjorie (McKinley) Buxton teaches a class on aircraft gunnery, Training Center, Memphis, Tennessee, April 1945 (Marjorie [McKinley] Buxton Collection, Women's Memorial Foundation Collection)

Lieutenant (junior grade) Harriet Ida Pickens, left, and Ensign Frances Wills, the first African-American WAVE officers to be commissioned. They were members of the final graduating class at the Naval Reserve Midshipmen's School (WR), Northampton, Massachusetts, December 1944 (National Archives, 80-G-297449)

Control Tower Specialists Third Class Catherine S. Pinzhoffer and Lovel Leeds give directions to pilots coming in for a landing, Naval Air Station Anacostia, Washington, DC, March 1945 (National Archives)

WAVES, carrying their full sea bags, leave the US Naval Training Station, Great Lakes, Illinois, after graduating from boot camp, World War II (US Navy photo, Mary [Hollenbeck] Myers Collection, Gift of Linda Reinhardt, Women's Memorial Foundation Collection)

WAVES Blanche (Fried) Arons and Helen Whittlesey in the control tower, Naval Air Station New York, Floyd Bennett Field, New York, New York, 1944 (Blanche [Fried] Arons Collection, Women's Memorial Foundation Collection)

This picture was taken after the dramatic rescue of Navy nurse prisoners of war (POWs) from Los Banos Internment Camp, the Philippines, on February 23, 1945. Vice Admiral Thomas C. Kincaid, USN, Commander 7th Fleet and Southwest Pacific Force, welcomed Navy nurses upon their return to American safety with our forces. The nurses received Bronze Star Medals in a nationwide presentation, September 4, 1945. Pictured left to right: Lt. Susie J. Pitcher, Lt. Dorothy Still Danner, Mrs. Basilia Steward (officer's wife), Lt. Goldia A. O'Haver Merrill, Lt. Eldene E. Paige, Vice Admiral Kincaid, Lt. Mary F. Chapman Hays, Lt. Cmdr. Laura M. Cobb (chief nurse), Miss Maureen Davis Tasic (civilian nurse), Lt. Mary Rose Harrington Nelson, Lt. Helen C. Gorzelanski Hunter, Lt. Bertha R. Evans St. Pierre, Lt. Margaret A. Nash, Miss Helen Grant (British nurse), and Lt. Edwina Todd. (US Navy Bureau of Medicine and Surgery Archives)

Navy flight nurses Ensign Viola Meining, foreground, and Lieutenant Thelma Reiling try their skill at adjusting litter straps on a NATS (Naval Air Transport Service) Skymaster evacuation plane at Naval Air Station Honolulu, Hawaii, April 1945 (US Navy photo, Omilo [Halder] Jensen Collection, Women's Memorial Foundation Collection)

Dr. (Lt. Cmdr.) Schirmer receives records and reports of patients from Navy flight nurse Lt. (junior grade) Viola Meining after air evacuation hop from Okinawa, Japan, to Guam, via Naval Air Transport Service (NATS), August 1945 (National Archives, 80-G-1350)

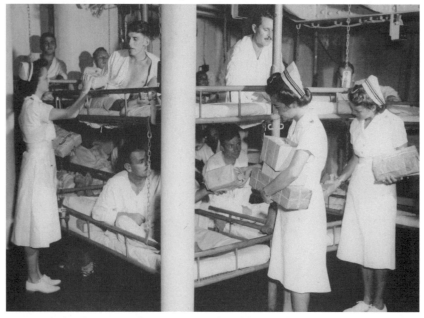

Navy nurses distribute care packages to patients aboard the Navy hospital ship USS Bountiful, circa 1945 (US Navy photo, Nona [Hambright] Vay Collection, Women's Memorial Foundation Collection)

Women Marines translate shortwave code messages, Marine Corps Air Station, Cherry Point, North Carolina, April 1945 (National Archives, 86-WWT-59-5)

Corporal Viola A. Eastman, Chippewa American Indian Marine Corps Women Reservist, Marine Corps Air Station, El Toro, California, 1944 (US Marine Corps photo)

Women Marine Privates Bette Wimer, Betty West, and Reba Fitzgerald repair an airplane engine, Assembly and Repair School, US Marine Corps Air Station, Cherry Point, North Carolina, 1945 (US Marine Corps photo, LaVeta [Edge] Francis Collection, Women's Memorial Foundation Collection)

Woman Marine Marcae (Bitowf) Carolan teaches a class at Radio Radar Section, Marine Corps Air Station, Mojave, California, May 1945 (US Marine Corps photo, Marcae [Bitowf] Carolan Collection, Women's Memorial Foundation)

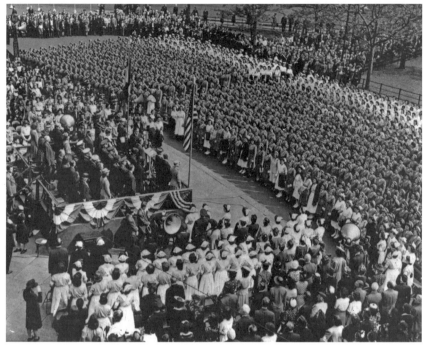

Newly inducted members of the US Public Health Service Cadet Nurse Corps stand at attention as the National Anthem is played during ceremonies at the City Hall Plaza in New York City. Fiorello H. LaGuardia (left of the speaker at the front of the rostrum), Mayor of New York City, administered the induction pledge to 1,300 new members. The event was part of a nationwide program marking the induction of 95,000 cadet nurses into the US Public Health Service, May 16, 1944 (National Archives, 208-MO-122K-1)

US Public Health Service Cadet Nurse Corps nurses, Sioux Valley Hospital, Sioux Falls, South Dakota, 1943. Seated left to right: Maxine Spear Norlin, Betty Hafer Nash, Hilda Hammanan Faber, Geraldine Olson Cheek, Genevieve Larson Miller. Standing left to right: Grace Sorenson Biggs, Elnore Schmahl Frentz, Edith Mussler Elwood, Esther Vander Berg Anderson, Margaret Hammah Roberts, Dorothy Stone Vandersour, Helen Schmuck Gamsby, Jean Davison Leary, Ruth JoAnn Cleveland Peters, Doris Rae (Maxine [Spear] Norlin Collection, Women's Memorial Foundation Collection)

US Coast Guard SPAR Drum and Bugle Corps, Washington, DC, World War II (Julia Sachno Collection, Gift of Judy Gaitan, Women's Memorial Foundation Collection)

The Coast Guard opened the SPARS (from the Coast Guard motto "Semper Paratus—Always Ready") to African-American women on October 20, 1944, but only a few actually enlisted. Pictured are two of the first four women to enlist in 1944: Olivia Hooker and Aileen Cooke (US Coast Guard photo)

Regimental Review, US Coast Guard Training Station, Palm Beach, Florida, World War II (US Coast Guard photo, Dorothy Nims-Klutz Collection, Women's Memorial Foundation Collection)

US Coast Guard SPARs Margery Small and Mary Demarinis christen the boxcar that will travel all over the country bearing the slogan "Don't Be a Spare—Be a SPAR," World War II (National Archives)

Chapter 13
Elaine Danforth Harmon, WASP

The year was 1939. Co-ed Elaine Danforth (Harmon) was a senior at the University of Maryland majoring in bacteriology. She was on the cheerleading squad, the rifle team, and the fencing team. She served as an officer in her sorority and was dating her future husband. Despite all this, she was bored.

Then an article in the university's newspaper, *The Diamondback*, caught her eye. The US government's Civilian Pilot Training Program (CPT) was seeking applicants for flight training at the College Park Airport across the street from campus. If accepted into the program, trainees would receive thirty-five hours of flight time, insurance, and, upon successful completion, a pilot's license. The cost was $40.

"Carpe diem," which means "seize the day," was Elaine's motto and how she lived her life. She knew this was the opportunity of a lifetime. At nineteen years old, she was underage, so she needed the signature of a parent on her application. Knowing her mother would never approve of her doing such an "unladylike" thing, she wrote her father at his dental office and asked him to provide parental consent and a $40 check for the pilot training course. He signed the form and dropped it in the mail the next day along with a check. With her father's permission in hand, Elaine submitted her application. The program accepted one woman for every ten men in the class. Elaine was thrilled when she received the news that she had been accepted.

All of a sudden, her senior year was not so boring. She worked hard completing the flight school, getting her thirty-five hours of flight time, and earning her civilian pilot's license.

After graduating from the University of Maryland and marrying her college sweetheart, Elaine worked in her trained field of bacteriology, but she found the work dull. The United States had entered World War II at this point, and everyone was looking for a meaningful way to contribute to the war effort. Jobs that were traditionally closed to women suddenly became available because of the war. Women went to work in factories to build planes, assemble military equipment, and take over when men were called to military duty.

An article in the July 19, 1943, issue of *LIFE* magazine about "girl pilots"—the WASPs, Women Airforce Service Pilots—got her attention. The Army Air Force needed pilots so badly, they were hiring women. The WASP program had been formed so female pilots could fly domestic missions for the Army Air Force, freeing up male pilots for combat. News of this opportunity for women spread like wildfire. Over 25,000 women applied, 1,830 were accepted, and 1,074 earned their wings.

Elaine's husband was due to head to the Pacific for an assignment repairing military aircraft. When she told him about the WASPs, he encouraged her to follow her dreams and apply. She was overjoyed when she received notification that she had been accepted into the program. It had been a couple of years since she had flown, so Elaine returned to the College Park Airport and brushed up with a few additional hours of flight time.

A telegraph arrived on April 7, 1944, with official orders from Jacqueline Cochran, director of the WASP program, and Henry "Hap" Arnold, commanding general of the Army Air Forces. Elaine was to report to Avenger Field in Sweetwater, Texas. She checked into the Bluebonnet Hotel. The next day she caught the bus at 9:30 a.m. and reported for training as a member of the WASP Class 44-W-9. The women came from many different ways of life, from farm girls to debutantes, but they all had one thing in common—they loved to fly. Elaine wrote in her dairy after the first day of training, "We were informed that we were being offered the most wonderful opportunity ever offered to women and to take advantage of it."

Training consisted of six months of ground school and flight training. The WASPs received the same training as the Army's male cadets with the exception of gunnery and formation flying, which were both considered unnecessary for their domestic military flying missions. The WASPs wore uniforms and conformed to military procedures and courtesies during their training.

Elaine Danforth Harmon sitting on the wing of a Stearman PT-17 during training at Avenger Field, Sweetwater, Texas, 1944. (Courtesy Elaine Harmon Collection)

Elaine Harmon in her WASP uniform, 1944 (Courtesy Elaine Harmon Collection)

On a typical day, Elaine rose at 6:00 a.m. to reveille, made her bed the Army way, and then marched off to breakfast. Everywhere they went, the WASPs sang at the top of their voices. The class was divided in half, each group called a "flight." After breakfast, Elaine and her flight reported for calisthenics and then to ground school, with afternoons on the flight line. The other flight would do the opposite and spend the morning on the flight line and the afternoon in calisthenics and ground school. This schedule was rotated every other day; if your flight was on the flight line one morning, you would go to ground school the following morning. Nights were spent studying or on night-flying assignments. Everything in Elaine's life revolved around flying while in Sweetwater. Taps, or bedtime, was at 10:00 p.m.

Ground school covered such topics as math, physics, navigation, Morse code, airplane structure, hydraulics, maps and charts, electronics, instruments, first aid, aerial photography, communications, aerodynamics, meteorology, Army and aviation forms and procedures, and maintenance and operations. Flight training was broken down into three parts: seventy hours of primary training in the Stearman PT-17, seventy hours of advanced training in the AT-6 Texan, and lessons with a link trainer to learn the procedures of instrument flying. Over time, Elaine learned spins and loops, slow rolls, snap rolls, chandelles, and the military application of these maneuvers and other aerobatics.

Even though these women already had civilian pilot's licenses, they had to fly with an instructor for eight hours before they could solo. On Elaine's first solo flight, she noticed something shiny in the fountain they called the Wishing Well as she came in to land. Later, upon investigation, she found that it was a quarter. She considered it good luck and had a hole drilled in it. She wore it on her dog tags, where it remains to this day.

Elaine's primary instructor was Rigdon Edwards. The trainees thought the world of him. Elaine gave Rigdon much credit for helping her through flight school, much as a coach might help an athlete. After her first solo flight, he gave her a candy bar. She ate the candy bar but saved the wrapper in a scrapbook.

Elaine always tried to do her best, work hard, and stay out of trouble. She felt a deep sense of responsibility to put her best foot forward for

Elaine Harmon in her pilot's uniform, 1944 (Courtesy Elaine Harmon Collection)

the women who would come after her. Still, she also had her fun while flying. But one afternoon, she was flying solo over Munday, Texas. She knew a family there that had hosted her and several other WASPs for a weekend between training phases. Elaine decided she had to buzz, or fly low over, their house even if she got in trouble for it. It was so much fun, she did it again. As she went in for a third time, she was surprised to see an instructor wave her back to base. She believed she would be dismissed.

Fortunately, they were not able to identify that Elaine was the pilot who had done this. She never came under suspicion due to her record of always following the rules. She was relieved to have escaped disciplinary action or possible "washing out" of the program, which was always on her mind. Elaine discovered many years later that all the WASPs were worried about washing out for one reason or another, though they never talked about it during training.

After earning her official silver wings on November 6, 1944, Elaine and her classmate Maggie Gee—one of only two Chinese American women accepted as WASPs—received orders to the Las Vegas Army Airfield in Nevada, known today as Nellis Air Force Base. They served as flight instructors for male pilots getting their instrument training. Elaine said it was her job to keep the men from flying into Mount Charleston while they were "under the hood." (A hood is used to restrict a pilot's visibility outside of the cockpit and allows the student pilot to practice flight maneuvers by referencing only instruments. The instructor pilot is in the plane with the student during this training.) While at Nellis, Elaine also logged time as a copilot in the B-17 Flying Fortress. Maggie Gee became a great and lifelong friend. Elaine was also close with classmates Helen "Casey" Cannon, Jean Downey Harman, Ruth Groves Kearny, Anita Bronken Matthew, Barbara Hershey Tucker, and Mildred House Ferree.

Fellow classmates were assigned other domestic military missions including ferrying planes, testing new planes, and flying planes from manufacturing sites to military training bases or to overseas departure points. They also flew planes with new engines for the required minimum hours prior to their entry into service. In addition, they tested, repaired, or modified planes before they were put back into service. They towed targets for artillery practice and for air-to-air gunnery practice where live ammunition was used. They transported personnel, acted as copilots for male officers logging their required flight time, and flew cargo missions— some of which were classified top secret.

During their two-year program these aviation pioneers delivered 102,000 aircraft and flew over 60 million miles on every type of mission and in all seventy-seven types of planes the military had in their inventory in defense of America's freedom. These planes included the P-51 Mustang, the B-17 Flying Fortress, the B-29 Super Fortress, and the YP-59A jet. Their flight assignments were military missions and included those not given to civilian male pilots who were under contract with private companies. The WASPs loved to fly; they were proud of their record and honored to serve their country. They proved themselves rugged enough to do it the "Army way." Thirty-eight WASPs died in service: eleven in training and twenty-seven more while on missions. Two were in Elaine's class.

When Elaine began her service, she had been promised that the WASPs would be militarized and commissioned as officers. When the first WASPs were assembled on November 18, 1942, legislation giving them complete military status was pending in Congress. This was still the case in 1944. In the meantime, Elaine and her fellow pilots were accepted as federal employees on temporary civil service status. With militarization pending, the WASPs were, in fact, militarized in every aspect of their training and operational duties.

One cannot imagine the disappointment when on December 20, 1944, the WASP program was quietly and unceremoniously disbanded, promises unfulfilled. Little or no official explanation for dissolving the program was given other than statements from Jacqueline Cochran and General Arnold that the pilot shortage no longer existed as the tide of war was changing and the "experiment" of a women's pilot program had been successful.

In his farewell address on December 7, 1944, to the last WASP graduating class (44-W-10), General Arnold stated, "You and more than 900 of your sisters have shown you can fly wingtip to wingtip with your brothers . . . It is on record that women can fly as well as men. I salute you . . . We of the Army Air Force are proud of you. We will never forget our debt to you."

But forget they did. The WASPs' story became a missing chapter in the history of the Air Force, the history of aviation, and the history of the United States of America.

Elaine and her fellow pilots received commendations from their commanding officers and honorable discharges from the Army Air Force. They were ordered not to discuss the militarization plans, and their records were sealed. Attitudes and cultural stereotypes of the time turned out to be the real culprit. Male civilian pilots working on government contracts for private companies were no longer needed in large numbers. They wanted the jobs that the WASPs were filling. With the help of the media and sexist stereotypes, an effective lobbying effort was launched to persuade Congress to kill the WASP militarization bill.

When the WASPs were disbanded, Elaine traveled to California and worked as an air traffic controller until the end of the war when her husband returned from the Pacific. When Japan announced they were surrendering, she celebrated with her husband in front of the St. Francis

Hotel on Union Square in San Francisco. They then moved back to Silver Springs, Maryland, where they built a little white house on a hill. There they raised their family of two sons and two daughters and pursued their American dream.

However, there is more to this story, and the first opportunity to tell it did not come until almost thirty-five years after World War II ended. In the mid-1970s, the military academies opened admission to females, and the news media began reporting incorrectly that these women would be the first to fly for the military. On August 9, 1977, the Air Force actually put out a press release saying, "for the first time the Air Force is allowing women to fly its aircraft." The WASPs' contributions to the war effort were not only going largely unrecognized—it was as if they had never existed.

Enough was enough. No longer under sanctions not to talk about their service, the WASPs began to speak publicly about their missions, the risks they took, and the losses they incurred. In 1975, Elaine was part of a core group of WASPs who organized to lobby Congress for veterans' benefits and acknowledgment of their place in history. They made their voices heard. Letters were written, phone calls were made, and testimony was given.

Elaine served as chair of the veterans committee for the WASPs and found herself giving testimony before Congress. With the help of Sen. Barry Goldwater, who had flown with the WASP ferry pilots, and Col. Bruce Arnold, son of Gen. Hap Arnold, they were able to get legislation passed by Congress. Pres. Jimmy Carter signed the G. I. Bill Improvement Act, Public Law 95-202, into law November 23, 1977, granting the WASPs what was intended to be full military status. It took another seven years for their medals (the World War II Victory Medal and the American Theater Ribbon/American Campaign Medal) to be delivered. Even then they were not presented in a ceremony but rather delivered in a brown paper envelope. Though the veterans' benefits were limited, what really mattered to the WASPs was that they now had the honor of calling themselves veterans.

With her newly recognized veteran status, Elaine found herself somewhat of a celebrity. She was an invited guest to numerous events recognizing World War II veterans. She received mail requesting photographs and her autograph. Teachers and children sent her letters, to which she responded with handwritten replies. She did book signings with authors who had written about the WASP program. Elaine particularly enjoyed it when she was invited to speak at schools. Preserving the WASP legacy was important to her, and this was a way to do it. It bothered her that they were not in the history books.

With official military recognition, Elaine was proud once again to wear her Santiago blue uniform—strictly according to regulation, of course. As a World War II veteran, she was now invited to many events commemorating what has become known as "the greatest generation." One of her granddaughters who lived nearby and frequently saw her in uniform has said, "It was normal for me to have a grandmother who had flown planes in World War II. When I was really little I thought all grandmothers were World War II pilots. I did not realize until I was older that she did all those volunteer speaking engagements in uniform not only for her love of service, but also as her way of continuing the legacy of the WASP."

Elaine and fellow WASPs Bee Haydu and Lorraine Rodgers were present in the Oval Office of the White House when Pres. Barack Obama signed Public Law 111-40 on July 1, 2009. Also present were active-duty United States Air Force pilots Col. Dawn Dunlop, Col. Bobbi Doorenbos, Lt. Col. Wendy Wasik, Maj. Kara Sandifur, Maj. Nicole Malachowski, and Rep. Ileana Ros-Lehtinen. Major Malachowski, the first female Thunderbird pilot, was responsible for initiating this bill to honor the WASPs. On March 10, 2010, the Congressional Gold Medal, the highest civilian award bestowed by Congress, was presented to the WASPs in a ceremony on Capitol Hill.

The bipartisan effort in Congress to recognize the contributions of the WASPs was led by Sens. Kay Bailey Hutchison (R-TX) and Barbara Mikulski (D-MD), and Reps. Ileana Ros-Lehtinen (R-FL) and Susan Davis (D-CA). One gold medal was cast and is on display at the Udvar-Hazy Center of the Smithsonian National Air and Space Museum. Each WASP or WASP family member received a bronze replica of the gold medal. Elaine donated her medal to the College Park Airport, where she first learned to fly. It is on display along with her uniform, silver wings, log books, and other personal items.

Elaine in a Stearman in 2010, just shy of her 90th birthday (Courtesy Elaine Harmon Collection)

Elaine Harmon at the 2010 Congressional Gold Medal Ceremony, Washington, DC (Courtesy Elaine Harmon Collection)

The face of the Congressional Gold Medal depicts the portrait of a WASP with three pilots in flight uniform in the foreground walking toward their aircraft, an AT-6. The aircraft, the pilot, and the feet of the three women pilots break the line of a circle around the medal, symbolizing crossing the boundaries and breaking through the barriers. The reverse side features three aircraft that are symbolic of the many types of military aircraft flown by WASP trainers, fighters, and bombers.

On April 21, 2015, Elaine Danforth Harmon took her final flight. Her wishes were to have her ashes placed in the Columbarium at Arlington Nation Cemetery. In complying with her request, the family applied to the cemetery for this honor that was awarded to most veterans with one day of active duty and an honorable discharge. They were stunned when the request was denied, as family members had attended a number of WASP funerals at Arlington in the past. Apparently, the Secretary of the Army had withdrawn authority from Arlington National Cemetery to provide inurnment of WASPs.

The family was thankful that this policy change had not come to light while Elaine was still alive. They were also extremely distressed at the thought of letting the fewer than 110 remaining WASPs and their families know that the battle for veteran's recognition was not over. The Army, the same branch of service whose call to duty these women had bravely answered, was denying them equal recognition with their male counterparts.

How do you fight the Army? Elaine's three granddaughters, Erin, Tiffany, and Whitney Miller, formed the perfect team. Tiffany Miller is a project director and women's history major. Whitney Miller, DVM, is a former Congressional lobbyist, and Erin Miller is an attorney and Twitter guru. This team turned to social media. Tiffany set up a petition on change.org. With tens of thousands of signatures, the petition attracted extensive media attention, followed by Congressional support. Whitney understood how to work with Congress, and Erin managed press relations like a pro. There was outrage at this injustice. As one of Elaine's granddaughter stated to the press, "The Army messed with the wrong family."

Congresswoman Martha McSally of Arizona, the first female combat pilot in the United States, stepped up and committed to making this right. She had been mentored by several WASPs throughout her Air Force career. She quickly introduced House Bill 4336, the WASP Arlington Inurnment

Restoration (A.I.R.) Act. Representative Mcsally's bill provides the same honor and recognition for these women veterans as their male counterparts.

Sen. Barbara Mikulski, also deeply disappointed by the Army's decision, sponsored the Senate companion bill, Senate 2437. In a statement released to the press, Senator Mikulski said, "If they were good enough to fly for our country, risk their lives, and earn the Congressional Gold Medal, they are good enough to be laid to rest at Arlington National Cemetery." Key supporters of this legislation included Sen. Joni Ernst of Iowa, Sen. Amy Klobuchar of Minnesota, and Rep. Susan Davis of California.

Three generations of Elaine's offspring stood in the wings as Congress voted on the bills. The House of Representatives passed H.R. 4336 unanimously on March 22, 2016. The bill likewise passed unanimously in the Senate on May 10, 2016. President Obama signed the bill into law as Public Law 114-158 on May 20, 2016. With passage of the

26 THE BALTIMORE SUN | SUNDAY, MAY 3, 2015   OBITUARIES

Elaine D. Harmon

University of Maryland graduate served with the Women's Airforce Service Pilots during World War II

BY FREDERICK N. RASMUSSEN
The Baltimore Sun

Elaine D. Harmon, who was a member of the Women's Airforce Service Pilots during World War II and later worked to gain veteran status for the pilots, died April 21 of complications from breast cancer at Casey House hospice center in Rockville. She was 95.

The daughter of Dr. Dave Danforth, a dentist, and Margaret Oliphant Danforth, a homemaker, Elaine Danforth was born and raised on 34th Street and graduated in 1936 from Eastern High School.

She became part of World War II aviation history in 1944 when she was accepted into the Women's Airforce Service Pilots — or WASPs — over the objections of her mother, who considered it "unladylike," said a granddaughter, Erin Miller of Silver Spring.

"When I began flight training, the school required at least one parent's signature," Mrs. Harmon told the Air Force Print News in a 2007 interview.

"Although my father was very supportive of my adventures, my mother was absolutely against the thought of me flying," she said.

"So I mailed the letter to my father's office. He promptly signed it and returned it in the next day's mail."

She had learned to fly while an undergraduate at the University of Maryland, College Park, where she earned a bachelor's degree in bacteriology in 1940.

She joined the Civil Aeronautics Authority Program and learned to fly Piper Cubs at College Park Airport.

Gen. Henry H. "Hap" Arnold established the WASP program in 1942. Its purpose was to train women as ferry pilots.

One of their jobs was to transport new planes from aircraft manufacturing plants to points where they were shipped off from overseas.

Mrs. Harmon was one of 25,000 women who applied for training. Only 1,830 were accepted, with 1,074 earning their wings. After completing the program, they were assigned to operational duties.

Training consisted of six months of ground school and flight training, with a minimum of 500 flight hours.

"She became a member of Class 44-9 and trained at Sweetwater, Texas, with a group of women that she always referred to as 'extraordinary,'" said Ms. Miller.

After completing her training in 1944 at Avenger Field, she was stationed at Nellis Air Base near Las Vegas.

During her career, she flew the AT-6 Texan, PT-17 trainer and BT-13 trainer, and was a co-pilot on the B-17 Flying Fortress.

In addition to delivering new planes, WASP pilots trained male pilots, ferried cargo, and dragged targets that were used for target practice.

During the war, 38 WASP pilots lost their lives. If a WASP was killed in the line of duty, she was not entitled to a military funeral, and her family was responsible for paying to have her body returned home.

They were not authorized to fly a gold star flag that meant a military death of a loved one had occurred, and they were

denied veteran status.

The WASP program was disbanded in December 1944.

After the program ended, Mrs. Harmon returned home to Silver Spring, where she lived with her husband, Robert Harmon, a He died in 1965.

All WASP records were classified and sealed for 35 years, which meant little was known of the WASPs' contributions during World War II.

"She said the reason the program was kept secret was because the government was afraid if enemy nations found out the USA was 'so desperate' to allow women to fly planes, it would be seen as a weakness," said Ms. Miller.

During the 1970s, Mrs. Harmon once again joined with other surviving WASP pilots in an effort aided by Sen. Barry Goldwater, who had been an Air Force pilot, to gain veteran status for them.

The culmination of their work was realized in 1977, when President Jimmy Carter signed legislation that granted the WASPs full military status for their wartime service.

In 1984, each WASP or a surviving family member was decorated with the World War II Victory Medal, and if they had served for more than a year, the various theater medals.

A final honor came for them in 2009 when President Barack Obama signed the bill awarding the Congressional Gold Medal to the pilots.

Mrs. Harmon accepted her decoration with other WASP pilots in a ceremony at the Capitol in 2010.

Mrs. Harmon continued flying and enjoyed taking her grandchildren up in small planes, her granddaughter said.

Mrs. Harmon attended WASP reunions in Texas and appeared at museum exhibits and memorial dedications.

She enjoyed speaking to schoolchildren and others about the WASPs' exploits and the role women played in the war.

Until nearly the end of her life, Mrs. Harmon would answer letters requesting autographed pictures of her in her WASP uniform.

Mrs. Harmon's WASP memorabilia is on display at the College Park Aviation Museum and on the Denton campus of Texas Women's University, which maintains a WASP collection.

She never lost her taste for adventure. She continued to travel abroad, played tennis until she was well into her 80s, and went bungee jumping in New Zealand when she turned 80.

Plans for funeral services, to be held at Arlington National Cemetery, are incomplete.

Mrs. Harmon is survived by two sons, Robert Harmon Jr. of Silver Spring and William Harmon of Ocean City, N.J.; two daughters, Terry Harmon of Silver Spring and Chris Harmon of Madison, Wis.; a sister, Jean Thompson of Accokeek; 11 other grandchildren; and five great-grandchildren.

fred.rasmussen@baltsun.com

Elaine Danforth Harmon worked to get veteran status for women pilots.

Elaine's obituary in the Baltimore Sun, 2015 (Courtesy Elaine Harmon Collection)

Women Air Force Service Pilot Arlington Inurnment Restoration Act, the legacy of these aviation pioneers is no longer at risk. The gates of Arlington National Cemetery will be open, and the WASPs will have their rightful place of honor in death on its hallowed grounds, never again to be forgotten. Elaine's ashes were laid to rest on September 7, 2016. This trailblazing woman was honored with a flag, military honors, a flyover, and a place in Arlington National Cemetery.

Elaine Harmon loved flying and she loved her country. Of her service she said, "It was a man's world. We were asked to do something extraordinary, and we did it." Carpe Diem.

Chapter 14
Martha Miller, US Army Nurse

Martha Miller was born in 1919 in Spokane, Washington, to an evangelist and his wife. As the third of ten children, she learned early to work hard and spent much of her time caring for her younger siblings. Nursing was a natural choice for her because of her love of people.

Graduating from nurses training shortly after the United States entered World War II, she joined the unit of nurses formed from her hospital. This unit became the well-known 20th General from General Hospital in Philadelphia, Pennsylvania. Commissioned a second lieutenant in the Army, she was shipped to the CBI (China, Burma, India) Theater and spent the next two and a half years on an Army air base in India on the Ledo Road, near the Chinese border.

The Ledo Road was built between 1942 and 1945 and connected the town of Ledo in India to the Burma Road in China. Military leaders felt the road was needed to protect China and Japan. It was used to move troops, supplies, and eventually an oil pipeline from India to China. When the Burma Road was cut off by the Japanese in 1942, the Ledo Road replaced it as a transportation route. Base hospitals, such as the one where Martha was assigned, were established along the Ledo Road to provide medical care to soldiers working near it. They were organized to Army standards with the assistance of the American Red Cross.

Beyond their quarters, the hospital, and its garden, the nurses usually did not venture out into the jungle. It consisted of matted undergrowth full of creatures. Besides the tigers, leopards, and snakes, the worst enemies were mosquitos, leeches, and mites.

Martha and the other nurses were housed in bashas, which were structures made chiefly of bamboo. There were three nurses' quarters on the base that housed a total of approximately forty nurses fit very tightly

2nd Lt. Martha Miller, US Army nurse (Courtesy Dean and Anne Whiteford)

Martha Miller outside the hospital of the 20th General Hospital Unit (Courtesy Dean and Anne Whiteford)

together. They slept on rope beds. The bashas had dirt floors and palm-frond roofs. The buildings' swinging doors did not latch, and sometimes animals—both wild and domestic—would wander in. It might be a jackal at night or a cow during the day. Because the electricity on the base was limited, they used kerosene lamps, which gave very little light. Fresh water was also scarce. Heat and fatigue tested the staff's physical limitations, but Martha was determined to try to bring cheer to this corner of the jungle. In the days leading up to Christmas, she helped to decorate the entrance of the ward for the Christmas holidays and the celebration of the Chinese Nationalist Day.

Sometimes the nurses would take trips to other air bases along the Ledo Road to deliver supplies, work, or visit. When they were off duty, they

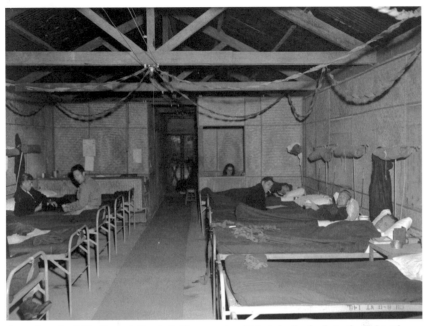

A ward at the 20th General Hospital. The nurse's cubicle is in the back to the right. The building has an inner lining of chatai mat, which helped both insulate and mosquito-proof it. (National Archives and Records Administration)

would sometimes travel in groups to visit a British club about two miles from their hospital near a tea plantation. Pilots would come from all over the jungle—as far as fifty miles—to visit with the nurses and dance with them for a couple of hours. Sometimes at night the nurses would play the card game Bridge. Martha enjoyed seeing the other air bases, especially as she sometimes saw the 1st American Volunteer Group, nicknamed the Flying Tigers. The Flying Tigers were a group of American fighter pilots that flew for China in late 1941 and the early part of 1942. Their planes, P-40s, are famous even today for their paintjobs; shark's teeth were painted on the nose of each plane.

The hospital staff often treated soldiers for tropical diseases. One of the worst was malaria, which was carried by mosquitoes, particularly after the monsoon season that lasted from July to October. Many of the staff were also infected with malaria and had to be treated themselves. The 20th General Hospital saw roughly 12,000 cases of the disease. Many nurses lost weight due to the extreme heat and working conditions. At one

On an inspection trip of Ledo Road installations, Maj. Gen. W.E.R. Covell lights a cigarette for an injured Chinese soldier at the 20th General Hospital (National Archives and Records Administration)

Martha steadying a table while a Chinese patient and Pvt. Trinidad Diaz hang decorations in the hospital, December 24, 1944 (National Archives and Records Administration)

point, Martha was told that she would have to be sent home if her weight dropped below 100 lbs. She was determined not to let that happen. Like the other nurses, she felt as though the boys needed her.

One of Martha's most memorable experiences was being assigned to Lord Mountbatten, 1st Earl Mountbatten of Burma. He had received an eye injury while inspecting British troops in North Burma, and Martha was his private nurse for one week while he healed. She was thrilled to learn that he was the second cousin to the king of England.

After two and a half years of selfless service to her country in Asia, Martha returned to the United States. She went back to college and met her future husband at church. He had been a B-17 navigator in the Pacific toward the end of the war. Shortly after their marriage, they moved to Massachusetts, where her husband enrolled at Harvard Medical School. He eventually became a thoracic surgeon. Martha has five children, seventeen grandchildren, and eighteen great-grandchildren. Now ninety-seven years old, she lives in Ohio with her oldest daughter, Anne, and son-in-law Dean.

Chapter 15
Dorothy Mae Wise, WAC

Women were first allowed to serve in the Army, under the Women's Army Auxiliary Corps (WAAC), in May of 1942. The primary purpose of a WAAC was to maintain stateside military operations, thus "freeing a man to fight" overseas. However, the corps was an auxiliary, meaning WAACs didn't have military status. In order to expand their use, the "auxiliary" was dropped from their name and the WAACs became the WACs, the Women's Army Corps, in May 1943. These women had the same rights and benefits of male soldiers.

Many women who joined the WACs sought to serve their country just as their friends, fathers, and brothers did. One such young lady was Dorothy Mae Wise. She was born in 1921 in Louisville, Ohio, to George V. Wise and Ethel S. Mercer. Dorothy had a younger brother named Edward and a younger sister named Elsie. On the eve of the war, she worked for the Hoover Company in North Canton, Ohio.

The Hoover Company made vacuum cleaners in the decades leading up to World War II. After the attack on Pearl Harbor, the United States began the process of converting industrial plants from peacetime manufacturing to wartime manufacturing. The War Production Board directed that all items considered nonessential should no longer be produced; the last Hoover vacuum cleaner came off the production line on April 30, 1942. After that, the company's men and women helped make fuses, incendiary-bomb parts, helmet liners, parachutes, propeller motors, and more. Dorothy worked in the ordnance assembly. She was one of millions of women who went to work in factories during the war. Many became known as Woman Ordnance Workers or, sometimes, "Rosies," referring to the government's famous "Rosie the Riveter" campaign to recruit women workers.

President Roosevelt signed the bill creating the Women's Army Auxiliary

Woman Ordnance Worker poster, 1942 (Courtesy US Army Women's Museum)

Corps on May 15, 1942. Shortly afterwards, the call went out encouraging American women to join. Within a few months, thousands had applied, including Dorothy Wise. She enlisted on August 29, 1942, and pinned on the Pallas Athene insignia, chosen by the first WAAC director as the symbol for the Corps. (Pallas Athene is the Greek goddess of war and wisdom.) Dorothy was sent to Fort Des Moines, Iowa, for training.

After a four-week basic course, she attended the cooks and bakers course. Shortly thereafter, she was assigned to the 1st WAAC Separate Battalion. At the time, neither she nor the other 198 women in the unit knew that they were a special company being formed and prepared for overseas duty. This would be the first time in history that a group made up entirely of Army women would be sent into a combat theater. Secrecy throughout the entire time of preparation was absolutely essential. In fact, the women were housed all the way across the post in cavalry stables that had been converted to barracks. They could not interact with anyone other than

Dorothy Mae Wise at the time of her enlistment in the Women's Army Auxiliary Corps, 1942 (Courtesy US Army Women's Museum)

those in their unit. The women practiced marching drills, how to use a gas mask, and additional training exercises.

Eventually, the women began to suspect that they were being prepared to be sent overseas, but still no official word to that effect was given. In the middle of the night in November 1942, they loaded Army trucks with all of their gear under complete silence and were taken to the train station. They boarded the trains and packed into boxcars for the long journey to a place only their officers knew about.

Two days later they arrived at their destination—Daytona Beach, Florida. It was there that they were informed they would be part of a newly formed unit, the 149th WAAC Post Headquarters Company. They would be sent overseas to support General Eisenhower's headquarters located in Algiers, Algeria. The women could not be ordered there, so they all had to volunteer. Dorothy Wise and the others eagerly agreed to go, unaware of the true adventure they were about to undertake. Weeks passed, seeming to drag on endlessly. Dorothy spent time with her new friends and was busy every day cooking meals for the WAACs. Just when the women began to think that the plan had been abandoned, they received orders on Christmas Day 1942.

Dorothy Wise's dog tag (Courtesy US Army Women's Museum)

WAACs on parade at Fort Des Moines, Iowa, 1942 (Courtesy of the US Army Women's Museum)

WAACs being trained to use their gas masks (Courtesy US Army Women's Museum)

Dorothy Wise (right) cooking at Daytona Beach, Florida, 1942 (Courtesy US Army Women's Museum)

They boarded trains again and were sent to Camp Kilmer, New Jersey. There they continued to wait. But this time their drills included carrying two large duffle bags strapped with web belts and canteens from point A to point B and back while wearing a steel pot helmet. This was necessary to prepare them for the hard part of boarding their troop ship. Finally, on January 13, 1943, they were trucked to the post on Staten Island, New York, and boarded the SS *Santa Paula,* a luxury cruise liner that had been converted to a troop transport ship. Gone were the nice staterooms and dining rooms—twelve women shared a room designed to carry four. They had twenty minutes to eat, standing up at tables. Very quickly, the ship food became difficult to swallow. They wore lifejackets all the time and learned to maneuver around with the bulky item around their neck.

They were part of a very large convoy of vessels led by the battleship USS *Texas.* There were more than thirty ships in the convoy, some troop ships and many destroyers. They arrived thirteen days later and docked at

149th Headquarters Company on the SS Santa Paula *on their way to North Africa, 1943*
(Courtesy US Army Women's Museum)

Oran, Algeria. Once off the ships, they boarded another train and arrived on January 27, 1943, to their new home at the Convent of Monasterte de Bon Pasteur, El-Biar, Algeria. Dorothy's parents did not know where she was or what she was doing. A letter was sent to them on January 28, 1943, signed by the WAAC director, Col. Oveta Culp Hobby, stating:

> "Dear Mr. and Mrs. Wise:
>
> Auxiliary Dorothy Wise left this letter with me to be mailed at the earliest possible moment and I am very happy now to be able to send it on to you."

Although the letter did not say where Dorothy was, it did give them her address. It was an APO, Army Post Office, in New York City. This meant she had been sent overseas. Not until Dorothy wrote home would they know her whereabouts.

For Dorothy, work began immediately. She was part of a group of ten that made up the cook and kitchen staff. She worked for S.Sgt. Gertrude Lund, who with the commander helped get the food supplies and supervised the cooking. The cook and kitchen staff worked twenty-four hours a day because they had to prepare meals for all shifts of all of the women in the office of the Allied Headquarters. Dorothy and the other WAACs worked seven days a week, with one half-day off to do laundry and write letters home. Eventually, they had the opportunity to visit the local shops and markets, where they were able to buy other necessities and souvenirs. Although there seemed to be some normalcy in their daily routines, they were nonetheless in a war zone.

One night shortly after they arrived, the air-raid sirens began to scream across the town to warn of an impending bombardment. Dorothy and the others were awaked by exploding shells around the convent. Everyone was scared and unsure if they would make it through the night. They later found out that much of what they heard were the Americans' anti-aircraft guns shooting at the German planes to protect them. This made them all feel better. On another night, shells did come through the convent ceiling, spreading plaster all over one of the beds. Until the Germans were defeated in Italy, the hazard continued.

Another enemy was the dreaded mosquito. Dorothy was issued mosquito netting to drape over her bed, as well as something called atrabrine. Every soldier was issued one of these small yellow pills at every meal and took it without asking questions. It was used to guard against the threat of malaria.

The WAACs were invited to take part in teas, receptions, and even parades. The French commandant, Gen. Henri Giraud lived in a beautiful summer palace. For one of the receptions there, Dorothy and the other cooks prepared lavish food served on china, crystal, and out of silver dishes. The Spahi, or Algerian Republican Guards, who protected the palace, wore brilliant uniforms. They rode white Arabian stallions; their horses would rear up, and the Spahi men would raise their swords up over their heads in a salute. Memories of this special day lived forever in the WAACs' memories.

Dorothy was given the opportunity to leave the Army and return home

WACs on parade at General Giraud's summer palace in Algiers, Algeria, 1943 (Courtesy US Army Women's Museum)

in July 1943 when the WAAC was changed to the WAC. She opted to stay in and remain overseas. The 149th WAC Headquarters Company was deactivated, and Dorothy and the others were transferred to the 6666th WAC Headquarters Company. Throughout the following months, large numbers of additional WACs were sent to Algeria in preparation for Operation Husky, the planned invasion of Sicily. The invasion was so successful that on September 8, 1943, Italy surrendered to the Allied Forces. The next focus became the liberation of France and the rest of the European continent. Everyone was busy, working hard to be ready for their next move. That Thanksgiving, Dorothy and the cook staff prepared a remarkable dinner that others later recollected as being one of the best. The cooks had a great reputation, and their meals became the envy of all the nearby units. Dorothy and the other cooks also prepared a special Christmas dinner of roast turkey, bread dressing, cranberry sauce, and sweet potatoes. Before long they learned that General Eisenhower was appointed the supreme commander of the Allied Expeditionary Forces and that his headquarters would be moving to England in preparation of the D-Day invasion. Many of the WACs hoped to be transferred with him, but only a few were chosen. The remainder stayed in Algeria until they were moved on to Italy.

Dorothy's unit was sent to the town of Caserta, Italy, near Naples. She remarked in a newspaper article that she had a wonderful view of Mount Vesuvius, which had erupted just a few months before. She was promoted to sergeant and became the head cook, in charge of the mess operations at the Army hospital in Italy. One day she had the surprise of her life. Her brother, Edward Wise, was a Merchant Marine third class. His boat docked in Tarento, Italy, on the Adriatic Sea. He knew Dorothy was near Naples on the Mediterranean Sea but he had to figure out a way to get to her to see her. He found out that a transport plane was headed there, so he went to hop a ride. But there were no seats available. He was told, though, that he could sit in the Jeep that was tied down in the plane. He jumped at the opportunity. This was the first time Dorothy and her brother had seen each other in ages. They had a delightful time catching up with one another.

By the spring of 1945, most of the original members of the 149th WAC Headquarters Company had finally headed home. Dorothy was flown with twenty-eight other WACs back to the United States in March 1945. She enjoyed a thirty-day furlough—the first break from Army work she had gotten since she left the States almost two and a half years before. In a newspaper article on her return to home in Canton, Ohio, she remarked that one of the highlights of her war experience was having had the opportunity to visit the great pyramids of Egypt on top of a camel. She also visited Athens and the island of Malta. After her month-long leave, she reported to Camp Atterbury, Indiana, for reassignment in the United States.

Women like Dorothy stepped up to perform an array of critical Army jobs in World War II. They worked in hundreds of fields such as cooking/baking, transportation, military intelligence, cryptography, parachute rigging, maintenance, and supply, to name a few. Through the course of the war, 150,000 American women served in the Army and were vital to

WACs sightseeing in North Africa, 1943 (Courtesy US Army Women's Museum)

the effort. The selfless sacrifice of Dorothy and other brave women ushered in economic and social changes that forever altered the role of women in American society.

Dorothy left the Women's Army Corps in the fall of 1945 and was married to Willard Chandler in January 1946. She had a daughter, Jeannie Chandler. It was Jeannie who donated Dorothy's uniform and documents to the US Army Women's Museum after her mother passed away in 1992. It is through these items that we are able to learn about the incredible journey and extraordinary sacrifice Dorothy made to support the war effort.

Chapter 16
The Call to Service

My service to the United States began in the mid-1980s when I accepted an Air Force Reserve Officer Training Corp scholarship to study at Georgetown University. I came from a family that was familiar with military service, including my father, who served in World War II. Many years had passed since that war, and the only two people in my family in the military at that time were my older sister and me. We were both ROTC cadets. As a third-generation American, I had strong desire to serve my country and see the world. That I did after a quick four years in college that resulted in my commissioning as a Distinguished Graduate in 1988. My first duty station was as an information management officer at Mather Air Force Base in California. It was in this assignment that I met and married my husband, who was an Air Force KC-135 navigator. At the end of this tour, I was given an amazing opportunity to study to receive my PhD in industrial/organizational psychology at one of the premier institutions in our country, Rice University. I accepted the challenge and after three years became a behavioral scientist in the Air Force.

When we received our next assignment, my husband decided to separate from the Air Force to pursue another career. I then worked for several years as a scientist at Wright-Patterson Air Force Base, the US Air Force Academy, and the Pentagon. I was then reassigned into the personnel career field and began many fulfilling years as a commander after attending Air Command and Staff College. I began my commander assignments at Davis-Monthan Air Force Base in Tucson, where I was able to witness firsthand the talents of the first female fighter pilot squadron commander, Lt. Col. Martha McSally. I was lucky enough to serve alongside Martha as a fellow squadron commander.

After serving as a squadron commander, I headed to school again at

Col. Cassie B. Barlow, USAF (Author's photo)

the Industrial College of the Armed Forces in Washington, DC. I was then afforded the opportunity to serve in my first joint assignment in the personnel directorate at the United States European Command in Stuttgart, Germany. After a short two-year assignment in Germany, I was again selected for command, this time at the group level, and was reassigned to Royal Air Force Base Lakenheath. I served airmen and their families for two amazing years in England. The time flew by and I found myself quickly looking at another assignment. I was headed back to a joint command billet, this time at US Northern Command and North American Aerospace Defense Command at Peterson Air Force Base. I was in charge of the personnel and manpower directorate. I was very excited to hear that I had an office in Cheyenne Mountain, where we regularly exercised our command's capabilities. After one quick year in Colorado, I was selected for wing command at Wright-Patterson AFB. There I was lucky enough to again be a part of a historic time for women, when the US Air Force selected and promoted its first female four-star general. General Wolfenbarger was chosen to be the commander of the Air Force Materiel Command and therefore was my boss.

Wing command is a highly coveted and very selective position in the Air Force that is offered to very few people. I was honored to be selected and serve airmen in that capacity. Wing command of Wright-Patterson AFB in Dayton, Ohio, was yet another very quick two years, and I decided at the end of this tour that it was time for my family and me to retire. I enjoyed every moment of my twenty-six years of service and would go back and do it all again if given the opportunity. It was a pleasure to serve alongside so many amazing Americans each and every day, and I'm immensely proud to have been a part of many historic moments in our US Air Force history.

Women have come a long way in the service of our country and have worked hard to earn a position right next to all of their brothers in arms. There were so many women who contributed to the current position women have earned in the US military. I wish I could have mentioned them all. This book is dedicated to all of those women who stepped up to serve our great country and who helped to achieve greatness for our amazing nation.

References and Books for Further Reading

Atwood, Kathryn. *Women Heroes of World War II: 26 Stories of Espionage, Sabotage, Resistance and Rescue.* Chicago: Chicago Review Press, 2011.

Bellafaire, Judith A. *The Army Nurse Corps: A Commemoration of World War II Service.* U.S. Army Center of Military History (USAMHI). http://www.history.army.mil/html/books/072/72-14/index.html.

Dalton, Curt. *Home Sweet Home Front: Dayton During World War II.* N.p., 2000.

Dalton, Curt. *Keeping the Secret: The Waves and NCR, Dayton, Ohio 1943-1946.* N.p., 1997.

Gruhzit-Hoyt, Olga. *They Also Served: American Women in World War II.* New York: Birch Lane Press, 1995.

"History of the 20th General Hospital in the China-Burma-India Theater during World War II." 2 vols. The Historical Unit. U.S. Army Medical Service. Forest Glen Section. Walter Reed Army Medical Center, Washington, DC, 1945. USAMHI.

Lloyd, Mark F. "Base Hospital No. 20." University Archives and Records Center, University of Pennsylvania University Archives. Feb. 1999. http://www.archives.UPenn.edu/histy/features/alum/99_2.html.

Miles, Rosalind, and Robin Cross. *Hell Hath No Fury: True Profiles of Women at War, From Antiquity to Iraq.* New York: Three Rivers Press, 2008.

Nathan, Amy. *Count on Us: American Women in the Military.* Washington, DC: National Geographic Society, 2004.

"U.S. Army 20th General Hospital Collection, 1932-1952 (bulk 1942-1945)." University of Pennsylvania, University Archives and Record Center. http://www.archives.UPenn.edu/faids/upc/upc15.html.

Yellin, Emily. *Our Mothers' War: American Women at Home and at the Front during World War II.* New York: Free Press, 2004.

Index